Reading is one of life's greatest pleasures. One can read in order to gather information or simply to be transported into a different time or place or experience. All too often I have found that "getting started" in the book is the biggest challenge, but once in I could stay engaged. When Lisa Baker began her book (and I love the subtitle: "written by Lisa Baker and lived by Marshall Brandon") I was anxious to see wait might come from her pen and from Marshall's heart. I have only had the opportunity to read a few opening chapters. To my delight I was captivated from the first page. I am looking forward to having the finished product in my hand. Lisa Baker is a gifted writer. She will transport you into the very soul of a man who has experienced life none of us are jealous for and a transformation everyone of us longs for. You will come to love and admire the man whose story she tells so vividly. But more, you will be drawn to the Savior who has gifted her and gave Marshall someplace to be somebody.

~ **DR. JAMES E. COLLEDGE**, founding pastor/ Christ Community Chapel

Someplace to be Somebody takes the reader on a journey of God's grace and the transformation of Marshall Brandon from a modern-day Saul into an incredible example of Paul. Marshall is set free from childhood abuse, drugs, imprisonment, rage, and hatred when he allows Jesus Christ into his life. From a life of despair to one with divine intervention, Pastor Brandon allows God to use his past to reach others with the good news they, too, can be set free. Don't wait to read this book about an incredible man with a remarkable story. Someplace to be Somebody will touch your life in ways you'll not forget as it has touched mine.

~ **EDWINA PERKINS**, Managing Editor of Harambee Press with Iron Stream Media/ Lighthouse Publishing of the Carolinas

———

I have met and worked with many writers—few have had both elements of a good book: a good story and a passion for writing. Lisa Loraine Baker has both. She was inspired by the story she had learned and she was absolutely committed to learning the often very puzzling and always challenging craft of writing a good book. Lisa was willing to go to any length to honor the story she knew had to get to its readers—and she did so. She is a dedicated student of story—and of writing itself.

~ **GINGER MORAN**, Writing Coach, Ph.D. Literature and Creative Writing, Author of Pushcart Editor's Choice nominee, The *Algebra of Snow* and most recently, *American Queen.*

As someone who's been in Christian ministry for over 50 years, I've made a lot of friends, and I've read a lot of books. But few have been like Marshall Brandon and Someplace to Be Somebody. Marshall has been a dear friend for over 30 years, but I never fully knew his backstory of God's amazing grace until I read this book. Marshall's journey goes from struggles with childhood abuse, to forming a gang as a teenager, to addiction and searing racism as a young soldier in Vietnam, and later imprisonment—and ultimately, to fruitful ministry. Marshall's story is one we all share: a search for acceptance and a place to belong. Someplace to Be Somebody is an inspiring story of how Christ's transformative power and grace can move someone from fighting and rage to kindness and love, from wandering and confusion to leadership and purpose.

~ **DAVE JOHNSON**, The Navigators, Senior Staff

SOMEPLACE
TO BE SOMEBODY

End Game Press books may be purchased in bulk at special discounts for sales promotion, corporate gifts, ministry, fund-raising, or educational purposes. Special editions can also be created to specifications. For details, contact Special Sales Dept., End Game Press, P.O. Box 206, Nesbit, MS 38651 or info@endgamepress.com.

Visit our website at www.endgamepress.com.

Library of Congress Control Number: 2021940945

ISBN: 978-1-63797-010-2
eBook ISBN: 978-1-63797-019-5

Cover and Interior Design by Greg Jackson, Thinkpen Design

Printed in India
10 9 8 7 6 5 4 3 2 1

SOMEPLACE
TO BE SOMEBODY

GOD'S STORY IN THE LIFE

OF MARSHALL BRANDON

Lisa Loraine Baker

To my Lord Jesus.
It's all about and for You.
—LISA LORAINE BAKER

———

To God Almighty for keeping me.
And to all He used to help me
be the person I am today.
—MARSHALL BRANDON

TABLE OF CONTENTS

CHAPTER ONE

THE WRATH OF RUTHIE

Marshall skipped toward home from half-day kindergarten. His normal route took him beside the soot-belching steel mills of 1953 Youngstown, Ohio. No puddle-dance that day as he zipped his oldest brother's hand-me-down coat to his neck to protect his gold-starred drawing from the dirty rain. The artwork, his first prized possession, depicted his brown-skinned family and their smiles etched in his imagination, smiles that belied their everyday reality.

"This will make Mom happy," he said to the early spring robins pulling on partially surfaced worms. He loved his mom and looked forward to her praise of his picture. He knew she would kiss his head and squeeze his cheek. Marshall *was* happy—until he walked into his home, the second floor of a house hastily built for the influx of ethnic steel workers during the Korean War.

"Wha—" His mouth clamped over the half-uttered word. His mom stood in the living room as she kissed a strange man. Marshall ran to his bedroom, the treasured artwork falling from his shaking hands onto the living-room floor.

There was no knock on his door, only hushed voices and the squeak of furniture. He quietly slipped under the sheets of the foldaway bed he shared with his four brothers and pressed his fists into his eye sockets, struggling to erase what he'd just seen. But the vision remained of his handsome Black mom in the arms of a darker, taller, Black man—darker and taller than his father.

Marshall fell asleep thinking, *Who is that man? Why was he kissing my mom?*

He woke to sounds of his father in the living room.

Is the guy gone? he wondered.

Marshall ran into the living room, eyeing his mother but heading straight to his dad, who sat on the sofa.

"Dad," he said, "where were you?"

"What you talking about, Boy? I was at work." His dad took a swig of his drink and rolled his eyes.

"But there was a man here…"

"What?" Edward Brandon glared at his wife and questioned Marshall. "What did you see?"

Marshall edged toward his room and stammered, "There was a man here, and he was kissing on Mom."

Edward jumped up; all attention now focused on Ruthie. The force of his lean, muscled legs pushed the sofa three feet back on the linoleum floor. He was a short man, but at that moment he looked like a giant to his son, who now cowered in the corner.

"Ruthie," he yelled, "you what? What's wrong with you, Woman? Why you having another man in the house? In *my house?*"

Ruthie said nothing. She stood and took the verbal beating, unlike her usual reaction. Marshall couldn't guess she had chosen her battle, and this time it wasn't with her husband.

"It was probably a guy you was messing with last weekend," Ed said as he grabbed his coat. He trampled on Marshall's unnoticed picture and on his son's heart as he slammed the wood door. He yanked the screen door so hard it stuck to the asphalt-shingled siding. The floors rattled as he careened down the steps.

"Daddy," Marshall blubbered, "where are you going? Daddy!"

As he stared at the door, he felt his mother's eyes on him. She turned and snatched something from behind the kitchen door. Marshall knew what she kept there. He saw her use it on his older brothers.

"Mama," he whimpered, "no." He stood still, not believing she would hurt him for telling the truth. He didn't know to run.

Ruthie Brandon wielded the extension cord like a whip. Frayed from repeated use, she used it for Marshall's first whuppin'.

Ruthie folded the cord in her raised fist and struck with practiced precision. The beating, lash after lash, was a vile act that shattered Marshall's innocent view of his mother. "Don't you ever tell him that again," she said. Her lips were so taut they disappeared into her face. Marshall looked at a stranger. This was not the same woman who lovingly kept his clothes clean and washed his hair. She yelled repeatedly as she continued to beat him. Marshall wailed as he became bruised and, finally, bloody. The weapon ripped his rumpled school clothes and tore at his skin. Every time he tried to raise his arms to protect himself, Ruthie grabbed them and hit him with even greater fierceness.

"Shut up," she said. "Stop that crying."

Marshall howled in pain.

"Just shut up, Boy," she said as she gripped his arm and propelled him into the living-room closet and slammed the door.

Marshall fell with a *whoomp* onto the bare floor of the closet. He tried to stop his tears and sniffed as he did. The sniffle brought a warning from his mother. "Shut up. You want some more?"

The small, dark closet seemed cavernous to the young boy whose only offense was telling the truth. The floor felt hard and cold, and the space empty, except for a few bare hangers, which swung from the rush of air when Ruthie cast Marshall into his new cell. Even so, he wanted to run into her arms and get the hugs she usually gave. With the physical and emotional battering, he crumpled into a far corner lest his mother hear him sniffling again.

He stopped his crying, knowing she would open the door and beat him again if he continued. Marshall lost track of time, and his legs cramped because of his stationary position—skinny butt on the floor and knees folded against his face. His mother finally opened the closet door and sent him to his bedroom. He limped as fast as he could to stay out of her reach in case she decided to whack him some more.

————

Edward and Ruthie Lansden Brandon married in Alabama when he reached sixteen and she a mere thirteen. The girl Edward said he stole away had their first child, Eva, in 1938, when she was sixteen. James (Abdul) followed in 1939, Will in 1942, and Watdell in 1944. Ruthie lost a set of twins before Marshall was born in 1948, and Willie Joe came along in 1952.

Ruthie lived like other Black women of the pre–civil rights South—her family as her source of inner strength in a society that still gave Black women little cause to celebrate. Black women were an unprotected group in the South, and many families sent their young women to points north and west for their safety. Since Ruthie married while young, perhaps having finished the eighth grade, her protection and escape from the confines of the South's racism came via her husband.

Her actions displayed a lack of self-esteem and inferiority—she, in the South, experienced the cruelest form of racism—she believed she didn't matter. Yet Ruthie rose above the stereotype and worked hard. She cleaned houses during weekdays and worked the polls for ten to fifteen years throughout Marshall's youth and teen years. She avoided interaction with the schools her children attended because she didn't read as well as she wanted. Nor did she count money well; she sent her children to the corner store to buy groceries. Marshall knew she kept her spending cash stuffed into her ample bosom under her bra. He felt the paper bills crackle when he got to snuggle with her. All her children knew her limitations and took advantage of them. Since household treats were rare, they used the change from grocery-store visits to buy candy, which they either ate on the way home or hid in their beds.

Edward was the youngest of eighteen children, born in 1915 Alabama when segregation ruled the land. One generation removed from slavery, he was the son of a man who had been born into captivity in 1859. Ed was a little man, about five feet, six inches and 120 pounds. He may have been small but was wiry with a considerable work ethic, which he carried to Youngstown, Ohio, in 1952, when Marshall was three years old.

Alabama in the forties was a land of separation. From hospitals to schools to water fountains, color segregated everything; such was the White majority's aversion to those of darker skin. In the hospitals, White nurses were barred from caring for Black, male patients. The city of Montgomery permitted Blacks to use the public golf course only one day a week. On railroad cars and city buses, areas designated "Whites only" separated them from Blacks, with Whites getting the preferred, up-front seating.

Black people fared no better in restaurants and service establishments. Entrances for "Blacks only" were relegated to the rear of buildings, with separate seating areas. Blacks who disregarded these segregation laws received heavy fines. All of this—the segregation, racism, and bigotry—led Edward to leave his southern home to be part of the Great Migration north. The period from about 1910 to 1970 saw six million Blacks move out of the rural South into the inner-city areas of the northern and western US. With their movement came a new culture, but it took years for them to settle in and begin to change the prejudice and racism that followed them northward.

Yet, unless they moved north, Ed's people thought they would forever be under the yoke of modern-day slavery, where Black men worked as or for sharecroppers. This thought kept running through their minds: *How do we get out of this?*

Edward went nowhere as a sharecropper's assistant because he served, in all respects, as an indentured servant. A person in that position never got out of the financial hole of constant debt to the landowner. Ed functioned as mostly unschooled labor, having completed only fourth or fifth grade. He, unlike Ruthie, could write his name, but he couldn't count well. When he picked cotton, he'd take it in and have it weighed, but he didn't know how to read the scale.

He trusted the merchant to be honest with him, but he was at a marked disadvantage. Going up north gave Ed the chance to make a life free from the weight the South made him carry.

Another landowner noticed Ed was a good worker and tried to entice Ed to come work for him. Ed's boss at the time built a cabin to encourage him to stay. But for Ed, as for many Black men in the South, there was little to keep him there. In the minds of Black men, the North offered a freedom they had yet to experience. Ed's cousin Willie had gone to Youngstown and, on visits back home, shared stories of the great jobs available in the northern steel mills. He coaxed Ed to go with him. After saving his money for about a year, Ed took his family north. At first the family lived with Willie in an efficiency apartment. Seven people in a small space is never palatable, but they made do. As soon as they could, the family moved into an apartment on the upper floor of a house.

———

Marshall's family was no different from other Black people who escaped the Jim Crow South to seek employment in the Steel Belt. The term *Jim Crow* came from a minstrel show entertainer performing in the mid-1860s, a White actor named Thomas Dartmouth "Daddy" Rice. He covered his face in Black greasepaint and created the character Jim Crow, his version of a slave. Sadly, the caricature was a bumbling imbecile. Jim Crow laws set up different rules for Blacks from those that governed

Whites, all to the detriment of Black people. During Reconstruction, southern Whites feared they would lose their jobs to free Black men, so the scurrilous laws were enacted.

Moving to the North meant, to the Brandons, a move to an emancipated life. But even in the North, where liberty indeed beckoned, racism persisted.

Their immediate neighborhood in Youngstown was known as the Monkey's Nest, a disparaging term used by White folks who lived elsewhere in the city. Those Blacks who escaped to the North were not as free as they expected. Prejudice still reigned, but they had more hope than they experienced in the South. Despite the name, the neighborhood was a peaceful community–a good place to live and work–with only an occasional party or family feud causing commotions.

This, the Caldwell area of the city, was what it always had been, a blue-collar neighborhood whose fortunes rose and fell with the steel industry. When the Brandons moved to the north side of Youngstown, the steel mills burgeoned as they helped supply the Korean War effort, drawing working men from many ethnicities. They all had to eat, so they all made it work, the local industry being their best hope. The mills permeated their lives just as the smoke enveloped the houses with its soot and smell.

Ed and Ruthie's apartment had two bedrooms, a kitchen, a living room, and one bathroom. Linoleum covered the floors, and Ruthie took great pains to keep it clean and waxed. She also scrubbed the woodwork each week in an effort to keep the soot that lingered at a minimum. The children's bedroom had a stationary bed that Marshall's older sister, Eva, used and a rollaway bed all the boys slept in and had to fold up each morning. Marshall's three older brothers bullied him throughout his childhood. Often, as they jostled in the bed for room, Marshall would wake with a foot in his face and a new bruise on his arm or leg.

The apartment's floors creaked, and with the uninsulated walls, cold air seeped into the place from fall through the next spring. One season, the Brandons' apartment lacked a major necessity: heat. That first Ohio winter for them was harsh, and Edward came home one day to a chilly house full of coal dust.

"Ruthie," Ed called to his wife, "why is it so cold in this place?"

"The furnace stopped working," Ruthie said, "and I can't find the landlord."

They had no idea if the furnace would ever get fixed or replaced—such signified the landlord's care of the place—so Ed bought a space heater and placed it in the living room as the sole source of warmth. At night, the children used their few blankets and body heat to keep snug. In the icy mornings, Marshall jockeyed with his siblings for space in front of the heater. Occasionally, he was so tired he fell asleep while he stood there, and his knees buckled into the red-hot metal. Those scars added to the ones inflicted by his brothers.

———

The steel mills were hard taskmasters, and the workers looked forward to their weekends off, relaxing and drinking with friends. Also, for Black people, escaping the South had not allowed the memories of overt racism to completely abate. Alcohol helped them forget for a while. When the Brandons' friends came over, they wanted diversion, a little fun, and a lot of liquor. Ed and Ruthie owned a console record player and radio combo, and they either found a favorite station or put on a record. All the couples paired off and, depending on the songs, either did a grind or a faster dance. The couples who joined for a grind found the slow and sensual dance a version of foreplay. Further intimacies either waited for later or happened somewhere in the house.

The older Brandon kids scattered as their parents' friends arrived each weekend. They tried to stay out of the way as they escaped to their friends' houses or out in the street. They knew when alcohol and dancing mixed, trouble followed. Marshall and Willie Joe were too young to be anywhere but home, so they stayed put in their bedroom. There, they looked through the keyhole, played games, and finally fell asleep.

When Ruthie drank along with their friends, the children knew she and Ed would fight, often with accusations, slaps, and flying fists and bottles. She abused her husband with a mouth full of vicious words and with her dukes, open as she slapped him and clenched into balls of fury as she beat on whatever he couldn't cover with his arms.

One weekend caused greater terror for young Marshall. Ed and Ruthie's friends were in the house and on the porch relaxing, drinking, and talking. Ed sidled up to a handsome woman and whispered into her ear, "Hey, baby. We need to get together. Give me your number." The woman grabbed some scratch paper and wrote her phone number on it. "Here you go, Ed. Call me anytime."

Ruthie watched the whole scene from the other side of the room and eyed Ed with disgust. Her ire didn't wait for their guests to leave. "You'd better enjoy that number because I'm going to make you eat it," Ruthie said as she headed toward Ed with her fists up.

Ed grinned as he balled up the offending invitation and popped it into his mouth. His smile vanished when Ruthie landed a blow on his shoulder while he chewed and swallowed the paper. He held up his hands to keep further blows away from his face as Ruthie continued to lash, slap, and hit him where she could. Ed never struck back; he held his hands up only to fend her off.

His attack came with words. "Stop it, Ruthie, just back off. You ain't got nothing worth fighting about. I know how you are. I know you mess around." Stung by his words, Ruthie struck again. "I'm getting a knife."

Ruthie ran to the kitchen and came back with the biggest knife they had, but by then, Ed had escaped down the outside steps. He didn't come home that night.

Though Marshall heard and witnessed the scene from behind his closed bedroom door through the keyhole, fear held him. The crowd dispersed as he trembled in his bed, Willie Joe long asleep beside him. The other kids stayed away from the house, and even though the bedroom door was shut, Marshall felt like he fended for himself in that madness. The fights didn't always start when people were there. When their company went home, Ruthie would often accuse Ed of some transgression. "I saw you talking with that ugly woman," Ruthie would say.

That led to them bad talking each other's mamas. "Your mama was so low-down mean, she looked up to a snake."

"Don't you say anything about my mama."

It escalated from there, and the brawls always began with Ruthie as the physical aggressor. She'd knock Ed upside the head and punch him wherever she could.

Neither seemed to care that the children witnessed their violent confrontations. When Marshall listened and watched through the keyhole and the gaps in the doorframe, he wanted to run, but the linoleum floors provided no quiet escape route through the sparse room. No rug existed to silence his footsteps dare he try to creep back onto his bed if the fight happened to spill into his sanctuary. Most times, he took his chances and ran to his bed as he tried to drown out the horrific sounds of trash talk, thrown bottles, and smashed glasses.

Marshall's childhood innocence and security eroded in the madness of his home life. He witnessed fights too often, which eroded his security. His safety relied on staying hidden because he couldn't run into the arms of parents-at-war who might miss each other and strike him.

He knew not to intervene because he would get slapped amid their unchecked violence. The stress of it often brought headaches. Many times, he told his sister, Eva, his head hurt so bad he thought it would bur st and his brains would fall out.

The usual post-party morning scene—spilled beer, wine-smeared floors, and bottle-littered tables—greeted the family after these weekend gatherings. As spotless as Ruthie tried to keep the house during her sober hours, on Monday mornings, it looked like she owned neither a mop nor a broom. The outside stairs and front porch often became spots for friends to sleep off his or her wasted condition. And so, the weekly routine began anew.

———

The weekend before Marshall started school typified the routine. He lay awake for hours the night before his first day of kindergarten. It was Sunday night, and the house was finally quiet after another drunken, raucous weekend. Saturday, when the "festivities" commenced, Marshall hid and remained out of sight for the duration either in his bedroom or the neighborhood. The bullets of slaps and verbal assaults fired between his parents ricocheted through the house.

As he lay in bed, he forced his thoughts to school—how his brothers and sisters had talked of the lifesaver it was. People were normal, and no alcohol was permitted. He finally dozed off and dreamed of the hope that school would be the escape he needed from the craziness at home. On the morning of his first school day, Marshall's excitement replaced his dread from the weekend of misery. Even with little sleep, he woke with expectation. He smiled at Eva as he sat up in bed. She was ten years his senior and like a second mom to him. She made up for what his mom lacked, a nurturing spirit without the animosity.

Eva was compliant—smart enough to listen to and obey her mom, whose temper was legendary within their family. Consequently, she didn't get beat by her mother. However, the older boys got whacked regularly with Ruthie's bare hands, the extension cord, or a lickin' stick she took great care to choose from an obliging tree. A narrow branch stripped of its leaves offered just the thing to use on a bare arm or leg. As the oldest child, Eva had some authority to discipline the boys, but Marshall was her pet, and she spoiled him.

That morning she helped Marshall get ready and walked him to the elementary school. Even in his excitement, Marshall felt nervous. His thoughts were all over the place: *Will I be safe there? Will it be fun? Will I like it? What will the teachers be like?*

As if she could read his mind, Eva looked at Marshall and said, "You'll be fine. Just listen to the teachers and do what they say."

"They won't beat me if I mess up, will they?" Marshall asked as he pressed closer to her.

Eva pulled him closer and reassured him, "No, Baby. You'll be fine."

After they reached his school and walked to his classroom, Eva gave him a hug and sent him in.

Marshall wasn't sure what he walked into, but he hoped for the magical place of knowledge his brothers and sister described so many times. His mother missed orientation, so he entered the school clueless. He started with half-day morning kindergarten, and his first interaction with his teacher was good, very good. When he met her, she enthralled him with her smile and warmth.

She looked at him and said, "Welcome to class, Marshall. We're glad you're here. Let's get you seated over here," leading him to a nice desk with a smooth, yellow top. He flinched at her touch but was delighted when she gently patted his back as he obediently sat.

Marshall took in the smell of the place, a clean aroma of wood, crayons, and paper. He marveled at his desk and the supplies he spied on the shelves. He owned no such things at home—no cognitive learning games or puzzles to stimulate his imagination.

This is heaven, he thought, as possibilities streamed into his mind. At home, when he wanted to draw, he used sticks in the dirt. He dared not write on the walls; he saw his brother get beat for doing that. In the classroom, he viewed all the crayons, paper, pencils, and glue to craft many things. He became as captivated with the potential that awaited him here as he had with his teacher. He looked at the other kids; some had supplies, which intimidated him. But when the teacher passed out pencils, he forgot his shame at having nothing. Everyone welcomed him, and he soon felt safe.

The first day flew by and, as Marshall walked home with his new pencil, he felt he owned the world and could do anything he set his mind to.

An intelligent young man, learning came easily to him in his first weeks of class. As he matched colors and shapes, he longed to discover more. He looked at the letters and numbers on the chalkboard and followed along as the teacher recited. He repeated each one and used his pencil and bright white sheet of paper to copy and learn the keys that unlocked this new kingdom of education.

It didn't take long for him to absorb the alphabet, and his teacher noted his intellect. "Marshall, you are a smart young man; you have a lot of potential and I'm happy to see you doing so well," she said.

English was his favorite subject, and an excellent memory aided his studies. At the time, his social and extroverted nature led him to make friends with little effort. He succeeded in school but not at home.

Even amid alcoholism, abuse, and adultery, Ruthie nurtured her children by making sure they had food to eat, clean clothes, and a ready and ample hug. They knew not to cross her, though; obedience was to be immediate and complete. After her initial blowup at Marshall, the beatings came at regular intervals, and Marshall always knew he'd done something to stoke her irritation. He figured she was still angry with him for squealing on her. When she hit him, she never backed down, much as she didn't with her husband.

Through all of this, Marshall's demeanor changed. He knew he had to get in line and stay there to avoid getting whupped. He learned what to do or not do to avoid her wrath—every act of anger brought her fists. A pout also reaped a beating, so he had to suck it up.

None of the children save Eva escaped the wrath of Ruthie. Most of the time, the boys were just being boys, and they acted up like young ones will. The children talked about it, and not one knew when she would go off on them. It happened when it happened. Marshall, being one of the youngest, got caught most often. He garnered her fury as the others escaped. When her temper rose, Marshall learned if he protested, she beat him; if he cried, she beat him; if he looked at her at all when she carried anger, she beat him. Not only could she throw a fist, but she could also throw objects with precision and force. If she couldn't catch him, she'd grab whatever was in her reach and propel it. She threw a jar of Noxzema like Joe Namath threw a football, and seldom did she miss Marshall's head.

He wouldn't win that war. If he whined to his brothers, he received their strong retorts, and they took out their abuse on him. Marshall grew a large chip on his shoulder and turned into an introvert. His hidden anger evolved in ugly directions as he grew older. His only sanctuary was school, although his studies started to suffer. Learning competed with his attempts to cover not only his bruises and broken skin but also his resentment at being abused.

His mother continued to have her boyfriend over while Ed worked, and the man tried to gain Marshall's favor by offering him money.

"C'mon, Boy. Let's be friends. Your mama likes me; you should too," he said as he tried to ply Marshall with a quarter.

"I don't want none of your money," Marshall said as he avoided the man's grasp. "Just leave me alone."

Ed still lived at the apartment, and not once did he mention the other man to Marshall. Marshall accepted his silence; he held more fear of his mother and what she might do should Ed bring it up. Marshall often came home to find his father laid out on the front porch, so drunk Marshall couldn't rouse him. He would shake him to no avail. Ed probably couldn't get up if he wanted to, and Marshall witnessed this drunken scene almost every day. A minimally functional drunk, Ed sobered up for his job but stayed in the bottle during his off time. Nonetheless, he never missed work because his value lay in his labor.

His father's uncaring attitude baffled Marshall. His young age prevented him from realizing Ed probably used the alcohol to assuage the pain from his past in the South and his present as part of a struggling relationship.

Ed grumbled a lot within earshot of his family, and he cussed out his children with the regularity of the whistle that signaled shift changes at the mill.

"You lowdown …" Ed added to the children's slang with his vulgar language. "Y'all are no good—won't be anything. You need to get out and get a job. You'll never finish school." Unlike the physical intimidation used by his wife, Ed didn't fight with anything but his limited, vicious vocabulary. Negative utterances persisted; his words often slurred from the booze. He'd talk to himself when he thought no one was around. Marshall heard him say more than once. "I need to get out of here; these people are no good."

Since Ed never fought back at Ruthie, he looked weak to Marshall.

Where is the man whose wife is cheating on him?

Why doesn't he stand up to Mom and make her stop messing around?

Where is the man who should defend us?

Where is the man who should treasure and affirm us?

Ed whipped Marshall only once, but it was nowhere near the hammering he got from Ruthie. Marshall just harrumphed at him, ashamed his father couldn't hold his own against a woman.

Ruthie didn't seem to care. She continued her affair and kept her children in lockstep with her discipline. How she kept her house dirt-free and her children clean and fed created a dichotomy compared to how she frightened them into submission. Marshall made a study of how to avoid her ongoing wrath, and he changed for the worse.

CHAPTER TWO

VISITING THE ROOTS OF RACISM

Between the ages of eight and thirteen, Marshall accompanied Eva and/or his mother on annual bus trips to visit relatives in Alabama. To Marshall, the whole experience was fun, mostly because it served as a break from the constant barrage of parry and thrust with his mother and his brothers. With either Eva's soft hand in his or with his mother's firm grip on his shoulders, they made their way to the Greyhound bus station, a two-mile walk from home along streets rutted with streetcar tracks. Marshall jumped on and off the tracks as they traversed the route, playing the part of a soldier fighting the enemy along an invisible front. War movies starring his new champions, John Wayne and Audie Murphy, became his favorite entertainment, and the long hike gave him opportunity to fantasize about a hero's life.

To Marshall, the bus terminal imitated an amusement park. He clung to his mom or sister as he embraced the dynamic environment. The loudspeakers regurgitated monotonous and blaring announcements to the people scurrying about. The clack of the ticket-punching machine provided a rhythm as they walked to their gate, and Marshall stared at the people of various sizes, shapes, and colors.

Seat selection proved easy when they departed Youngstown, but the Ohio River marked the Mason-Dixon line, and there, the rules changed.

Surveyed in the eighteenth century, the line came to be the demarcation between slave and free states. Even in the 1950s, the color barrier was solid. In Cincinnati, they changed buses and seat order. Black folks moved to the back and Whites took the front seats—the unfortunate Southern societal norm. In the bus stations, Eva or Ruthie always guided Marshall to the restrooms and drinking fountains marked *Colored* so he wouldn't inadvertently cause trouble. Marshall began to sense the changes on these trips as he grew into his teens. He saw and questioned the separate water fountains and restrooms, but Eva and Ruthie made sure he complied.

At eight years old, Marshall accompanied his mom on what would become a memorable trip for him. Ruthie kept him protectively close; Marshall enjoyed the contact and wished for a lot more of that side of her. He held on to her hand as they made their way through the mass of travelers. The fried chicken Ruthie made for their lunch greased their paper lunch sacks, and Marshall held his bag on the bottom in case it tore. He licked the residue from his fingers as an appetizer, even while eyeing vending machines filled with sugary temptations he could not buy.

As the bus headed south out of Cincinnati, only one seat remained for Marshall, in the wrong section, adjacent to a White lady. As Ruthie settled into her seat, Marshall stood and looked at the empty one.

"No, Child," said the White woman, "you can't sit here."

Marshall didn't budge because he feared what would happen if he didn't get a seat. He asked as politely as he could, "Ma'am, may I have this seat? There ain't any others on the bus."

"I told you no, Young Man. You just go on and stand in the aisle." Ruthie noticed the interaction and stood up to the White woman.

"You let my son sit down," Ruthie said.

The woman slid over and prevented Marshall from getting into the seat. "No!" Not to be handled by a White lady, Ruthie raised her voice, "Woman, you better move yourself and let this child sit down."

By then, the other passengers got engaged and shouted at Ruthie, Marshall, *and* the White woman.

The driver, all six feet, five inches of him, strode down the aisle and assessed the situation.

"Ma'am," he said as he looked at the White woman, "this bus ain't going nowhere until you let this little boy have a seat. We have a full load, and I'm sure the other passengers will appreciate it if you let him sit down so we can keep on our schedule."

The woman said nothing, slid over as close to the window as she could, and stared out at the parking lot.

Marshall looked at his mother for approval.

"Sit down Child, and don't cause any trouble by bothering this nice White lady," Ruthie whispered, then smiled. As she turned to take her seat, the White woman looked at her, and Ruthie harrumphed.

The bus ambled off, and the passengers settled in for the long ride. The drone of the engine, the gentle vibration of the wheels on the pavement, and the stress of the confrontation wearied Marshall. He started to slumber, but his head slumped against his hostile seatmate. He shuddered, and she recoiled but didn't push him away. Later, when Marshall woke up, he looked up and flinched as he realized he was still leaning on her. As he sat up, he yawned and looked back at his mother for moral support; she was two rows behind, eyes closed. The scent of leftover fried chicken made his stomach gurgle in anticipation. The accelerated trip through the Cincinnati terminal left him with a half-eaten lunch. He grabbed the lunch bag at his feet, pulled out the last piece of chicken, and polished it off as he used his sleeve as a napkin. He looked past the White woman, avoiding her eyes, and watched the landscape roll by as she smoothed her dress.

Owens Cross Roads, Alabama, hadn't changed much in the time since Marshall was born there. His mom and sister told him what it was like back in the days before they moved. A small burg of less than eight hundred people, south-southeast of Huntsville, Alabama, it sits near the

Tennessee River and owes its name to the Owens family of settlers of the mid-nineteenth century. Before a boll weevil infestation, the main source of employment was cotton farming, which had been Marshall's father's trade. Only a few pockets of cotton farms remained. Willie and Edward, the only two family members who departed, left many of the Brandons still living in the area.

On one of their trips to Owens Cross Roads, one of Ruthie's sisters won the coveted right to host the visitors from up north. Coming from an urban setting, Marshall thought the rural town quiet and a little backward. He was used to a 'hood with concrete streets, masses of cars and trucks, and, well, lots of everything. His birth town was stuck in the past, and prejudice was a fermented leftover.

"Marshall," said his aunt, "run down to the store and pick up some bread for us." She gave him a quarter, and he sauntered down the dirt road toward town. The air smoldered, and as he wiped the sweat from his neck, he dropped the quarter. He picked it up and cleaned the dust off with his shirt. His attention still on the quarter, he heedlessly walked into a store marked "Whites only." He met no one's gaze and grabbed the first loaf of bread he saw.

"Is that all you need?" the clerk said.

"Yessir," Marshall answered, and he smiled as he handed over his quarter.

With change in his pocket and a loaf of bread in his arms, Marshall headed back to his aunt's. Shortly after Marshall returned, another uncle who witnessed Marshall's infraction came into the house.

"Boy," he said to Marshall, "don't you know you're not supposed to go into that store where you bought the bread?"

"Sir? What'd I do wrong?"

"Son, that store is for Whites only. Don't be getting your family in trouble because you don't know how things work around here."

"Marshall Brandon," said his mother, "don't you ever go into that store again."

"But—" He was cut off by his mother. "Young man, that store is for Whites only. Don't ever do that again. You could get my sister in trouble."

"Yes, ma'am." Marshall cowered because he, at last, realized he had done something wrong.

Once Ruthie had said her peace, she let him be.

Marshall didn't repeat his mistake. Embarrassed, he didn't want to put his family in harm's way or incur a wrathful beating from his mother when they got home to Youngstown.

She held grudges.

That lesson in the ways of injustice stunned Marshall. He heard first-hand accounts of how things worked in the South from his family before, and they repeated the lessons so he wouldn't forget. Personal experience trumped stories. As Marshall grew, his introversion due to his unbalanced treatment at home morphed into a deep-seated anger—Southern racism exacerbated his homegrown issues.

The invisible war front Marshall fought on the tracks at home collided with reality.

CHAPTER THREE

ESCAPE TO THE STREETS

As Marshall matured, Ruthie sent him out to play while her man visited. Marshall complied and learned life on the street. He attended nickel movies and still admired John Wayne and Audie Murphy, heroes like his father would never be. His only other champions, the kids who taught him how to survive on the street, outdid his screen stars. Marshall roamed the neighborhood, but as he roamed, he got into fights because it helped release his anger.

He couldn't talk at home because his family didn't value his opinions. As he grew older and tried to talk with his mother, she often answered his questions with, "Shut up, you. Just shut up. Don't want to hear none of your trash."

As Marshall endured his mother's abuse and his brothers' torment, he turned from a bright, young student who loved school into a rage-filled recluse who looked for emotional and physical release.

Marshall knew how to fight. He learned defense beginning at age five when he had to fend off his brothers. He gained additional avoidance skills when he had to hide from his mother's rage. He received vicarious offensive training when he watched his mother beat on his father and direct experience when she beat on him. All of it robbed Marshall of a carefree childhood because he always stayed on guard, on defense, and ready for any adversary (real or perceived) who came at him.

Ruthie wielded fierce discipline at home, but when her children were out on their own, she taught them that if someone else started a fight, they were to defend themselves.

She only walloped them if they started the fight; otherwise, she stood by their actions.

"You'd better fight," Ruthie told her boys. "You'd better not start it, but you'd better defend yourself and finish it. Don't let me see anyone running you home." Her children would rather fight their antagonists than get beaten by their mother.

Marshall gained his props by how well he could fight. Small for a ten-year-old, he looked an easy mark to other kids, but they soon learned otherwise. Marshall tried to fend off his brothers, but when their mother was home, she defended him against them. If they picked on him then, they'd get it from her. None of the children got too big to ignore her rules.

Marshall always defended himself in a quick and brutal manner. His pain surfaced when he fought, and he fought to hurt. He would not take anything from anyone other than his mother. When she beat him, he resolved that no one else ever would. He vowed to challenge whoever came at him. Through it all, he loved his mother in the strange way an abused person often loves their abuser. He believed a man should love his mother, period.

On the way home from school one day, the White kid who lived down the street came at him with a toy cowboy pistol in his hand. He ran up to Marshall and coldcocked him on the back of his head. Marshall didn't pass out, but as he felt his head and looked at his hand, he saw blood.

He looked at the kid and said, "No one messes with me." *Only my mama is allowed to beat on me.* Marshall bashed the kid all the way up his driveway and to his house. Then Marshall beat feet home.

The kid squealed, and his mother brought her battered child to show Ruthie.

"Look what your son did to my child," the mother said.

"Did you do this?" Ruthie asked Marshall.

"Yes, ma'am, I did," said Marshall, who stood beside his mother.

Ruthie said, "Did you start it?"

"No, ma'am." Marshall told her what happened.

"You take your child home," Ruthie said to the astounded mother. The matter ended there.

Marshall knew his mother, in her own way, was proud of his ability to fight, to defend himself against others.

One of Marshall's insecurities stemmed from a single but regular thought: *How do I cover these bruises and cuts?* At six, he did his best to keep his wounds covered, cognizant of his shame if people knew his mom beat him. As he grew, fighting with others gave him a way to explain the marks left by her lashings.

By the time Marshall reached his early teens, the only brother who still lived at home to beat on him was the taller and heavier Watdell. He chose to intimidate Marshall just because he could. Marshall stayed out of his reach and ambushed him instead. Marshall threw rocks, bricks, or a bottle at Watdell's head. Or he'd get a knife and try to stab him or his other brothers if present. They had hurt him, and he wanted to do them harm. Killing them entered his mind; he'd become that hard. They'd wrestle the weapons from him, but they knew he'd get even eventually. When Marshall sensed they planned to gang up on him, he outran them.

As he got older, the abuse Marshall suffered from his brothers lessened, mostly because they knew he would fight back. And as Marshall's reputation as a street fighter increased, few homes welcomed him, save his own. Other kids would say, "You're just evil."

Marshall scrapped with other kids almost every day—all the way to school and all the way home—rarely getting a scratch. No one escaped him. A neighborhood family, whose mom everyone knew as Miss May, recognized his reputation. One day she staged a confrontation between Marshall and one of her boys. Miss May was angry that Marshall, smaller than her son, beat him. She later sicced her boys on Marshall as he walked by. She said to her kids, "You better get out there and fight." All the boys came out as one to defeat the infamous Marshall Brandon.

Marshall looked up and said, "Okay, here we go. Bring it on."

The three boys pounced on him, but they couldn't beat him. Marshall fought like a mad man, and not one of the boys was able to land a decent blow. Marshall hit, ducked, spit, and tripped them. Then Miss May did the almost unthinkable; she sent her daughter into the fight also. Marshall fought them all at the same time, beating them soundly. He walked away with the swagger he earned.

"Send a girl out to fight? Woman, what's your problem?"

Marshall's mother witnessed some of his fights, and at times she'd send Watdell out to help. But Marshall didn't want help; he needed to win on his own. If he got into a fight, he'd finish it himself, something he couldn't do when his mother beat him. He never raised a hand against her. Winning fights against others signified his statement of bravado, a sort of high five to his mother that he, too, could whup on somebody and win.

School had become less a sanctuary and more a platform of escape. Because his homelife stunk, his schoolwork suffered. He rarely brought assignments home because the effort to think through problems was overwhelmed by the bickering and bullying. He did what he had to do to get by, preferring to be on the streets with his buds. He also began to witness the unfairness of White authority at the school.

Marshall thought about getting involved in sports, but watching coaches berate and physically taunt the players was too much for him. He thought, *I get that at home; why should I get it from White people? I can't be under the authority of White men who kick their players.* He disengaged from school and began losing his potential.

Even though his interest waned, he continued to attend school because his report card would show that he hadn't. With Eva's help, Ruthie kept track of each child's school report card. Anything less than a passing grade garnered a beating. As bad as her beatings were, Marshall knew his mother wanted better for her children.

───────

At thirteen, Marshall started a gang. He also stopped making trips to Alabama with his family. In a group of fourteen guys called New Breed, he served as the president and his friend Lonnie, the vice president. It began as a social club, so the members would have like-minded mates to hang with. But if trouble befell any one of them, the others would stand up for him, no questions asked.

One day, apart from his gang, Marshall walked home from school clad in his cleated shoes. The flat, metal heel plates exclaimed, "Look out, I'm coming through!" Young men in that day wore them to sound cool and turn heads. As he walked, he met tough guy Mo, eighteen and in the eighth grade—a real scholar. Mo possessed no coolness; he just liked to fight. He excelled at it, often using trick tactics to overcome his opponents. This was his personal badge of authority in the 'hood.

Mo came at an unarmed Marshall that day with a knife, so Marshall ran to avoid getting stabbed. Cleats weren't known for their traction, and as Marshall ran, he tried to cut in between two cars, slipping under one. Mo caught up to him and started kicking Marshall in the face. Before he could use the knife, Mo was distracted long enough for Marshall to get out from under the car and run.

The next day Marshall strode back to Mo's turf with Lonnie and Weston, two other gang members. They armed themselves with sticks, tire irons, bats, and this time a knife. Marshall, now prepared to do battle, found Mo hanging with his friends.

"Mo," Marshall said as he stood, slapping a tire iron against his palm.

Mo's eyes got wide, but his friends were around, and he couldn't afford the drop in status. He stood his ground, albeit with group courage, the kind that comes when a guy knows he has backup.

He had that all wrong.

"You can't beat me now," Marshall said as he got busy on Mo. Lonnie and Weston kept Mo's friends from joining the fight because Marshall wanted to take care of him on his own. When Marshall and his guys left, Mo was on his knees, coughing and spitting. Marshall made his point, and Mo didn't bother him again.

Marshall had a few altercations at school but was always on defense against someone looking to make a name for himself by beating him. He did not claim nor wear the reputation as a bully. He rarely beat up someone for no reason, but he liked to rough up those who challenged him or beat up others who didn't deserve it. Marshall hated to see someone else suffer mistreatment. He could defeat even those older and bigger than him, so he surprised a lot of people. And he never took anyone's skills for granted, even the girls who came at him like a boy would. They all succumbed to Marshall's expertise.

One time Marshall got kicked out of class for stabbing another boy in the leg. Why did Marshall do it? Because the kid dared him. Sent to the principal's office, he faced the detectives who had gathered to get his story. Marshall refused to talk.

"What do you have to say for yourself, Marshall?" the principal said.

"Son," said one of the officers, "you may end up at the boy's industrial school if you don't settle down. Now, are you going to tell me what happened?"

Marshall told them the kid dared him to stab him. That ended the incident. But it wasn't the end of it as far as it concerned his mother, who got called to come in too. After the detectives left, the school psychologist came in. With his mother in the room, Marshall clammed up.

"Marshall, are you going to talk to me?" asked the psychologist.

Marshall remained silent.

The psychologist looked at Ruthie and said, "Until he talks to me, he's not going back to class."

His mother glared at him as he sat stock-still. He was so suppressed at home, he internalized his anger and refused to talk. A silent walk home resulted, except for the sound of Ruthie's determined steps as she grasped Marshall's collar and dragged him along.

Once they got home, Ruthie got the extension cord and said, "You are going to talk," and she pummeled him into a bloody mess. For almost an hour, she beat him and spewed her venom.

He didn't cry anymore when she beat him; instead, he balled his fists and bit his lip. That time he bit it so hard it bled. Only when he promised to meet with the school psych (as he called her) did she stop.

When the meeting took place, Marshall sat across from the psychologist. His mother did not attend. He displayed false bravado and refused to talk for a while until he thought of what his mom would do to him if he didn't.

"Okay, I'll talk. What do you want to talk about?" he finally said. He told her about how the other kid dared him to stab him, but he revealed nothing about his home life. That subject—a family thing—he refused to broach. Once he told his side of the story, the case was closed. She wrote out a permission slip and sent him back to class.

He thought about the detective's threat. *Boy's industrial school. Oof! That's just another name for prison. I think I'd rather face my mother.* He knew guys who'd been sent to that school, and they shared horror stories of their treatment there. He wanted no part of it, so he acted cool and did his best to avoid being sent away.

Ordinary days for Marshall consisted of jabs and ducks as he tried to find some stability in the madness of his family life and the rage that encompassed him. Soon he would reach a tipping point where his options gave him only one way out.

CHAPTER FOUR

ENOUGH!

Marshall's abuse at the hands of his mother stopped when he turned fifteen. By that age he proved himself to his peers and his brothers; the time came for him to stand up to her. At last, the moment came when he determined not to take any more. He'd developed a tough crust, and she could no longer break it.

On that day, he tried to talk to her, but all she said was, "Shut up. You don't have an opinion, just shut up."

"Mom, just talk to me."

She picked up the closest thing she could find—a bottle—and threw it at him. Along with his toughness, Marshall became adept at dealing with this side of Ruthie. He caught the projectile and held it, wondering if he should throw it back at her. Lord knew, he wanted to. He marveled that he finally might have the upper hand. He almost boomeranged the bottle, but instead, he started to smile, which made her angrier.

"You evil child," she said.

Marshall clammed up, much like he often did when she came at him with abusive words.

Ruthie had the extension cord within reach wherever she was in the apartment, almost like an appendage. She grabbed it and wound the unfrayed end around her wrist, leaving the scourging end free to flail on him. She lunged toward her son.

"And what do you think you're going to do?" Marshall smirked, raising his hands.

"I'm going to crack your skull, you no-account street boy." But her eyes grew wide because as she came at him, his smile broadened. She grimaced but still raised her arm, and the cord came up off the floor. As she drew back her arm, the cord flew up and behind her, ready to strike Marshall.

Before Ruthie could slash out, however, he grabbed her wrist and stopped her. As she raised her other fist to bash him, he grabbed it too. Their eyes locked—his cocked and wary, hers sharklike, no whites showing.

"C'mon, Baby, you're not going to hurt me anymore. I ain't taking one more lick," Marshall said as he softened his grip. He held her wrists with a reluctant tenderness because, in his heart, he wanted to strike. He wanted to repay her for all the years of abuse.

He thought, *How can anyone who does this say they love me?*

It took enormous restraint to stand there and wait for her eyes to focus—to get past the blinding animosity. Her beatings almost eclipsed all the affection she had ever shown him, and he waited. He reflected on the tenderness she had shown through the years—the love he needed was not the love that manifested itself as clean clothes and a sack lunch. When the hugs and snuggles he relished as a child were replaced by animosity, it became hard for him to remember being cherished, and yet he knew he had been, once. He did not hit her or yell at her—the waiting served his purpose of letting the role reversal sink in. He stood immovable, now in charge.

They may have remained there for a full sixty seconds, an eternity when rage is in the mix. But Marshall determined to make her hear him, and he wished to wear her down, no matter how long it took. When her eyes cleared, he acknowledged her with a nod of his head and a stiff upper lip. He couldn't offer a full-fledged smile quite yet; she had to earn his trust.

When she finally tried to pull her wrists from his grasp, he asked, "Mom, are you done?"

She looked at him, transfixed by the one son who made a clear departure from the norm. He alone stood up to her. The others always fled. And then Marshall saw a tear form at the corner of one of her eyes. She looked down, and her whole body became like a rag in his hands. Maybe the years of the harm she inflicted finally deflated her. He still held her wrists, lest she change her mind, but as she started to cry, he discovered, to his surprise, tears in his own eyes. He felt no forgiveness, just relief that the moment was over.

"Mama. Don't ever come at me again. You hear me? We are past that," Marshall said. She remained silent, but her tears spoke the apology he needed. There was no hug, but they cried together in acknowledgment of Marshall's manhood, a strong man who would not take her offenses anymore. Those days ended there.

Marshall won freedom from his mother's physical punishment, but his soul bore the damage, and mental anguish remained. Although he and his mother were now cool with one another—she showed a healthy respect for him since he stood up to her, and he showed her wary courtesy in return—his father's oblivion and drunken stupor remained. By the time he was seventeen, Marshall's nurturer—his twenty-seven-year-old sister, Eva—enjoyed a busy life as a wife and mother of a three-year-old and one-year-old. Marshall's oldest brothers, Abdul and Will, each quit school and moved out of the house. Watdell also quit school, but still used the family home as temporary quarters when whichever woman he lived with put him out. At that time, Watdell fancied himself a pimp and a player. Marshall and the youngest Brandon, seventh-grader Willie Joe, were the only children living full-time in the Brandon household.

Ruthie continued to debase her marriage with her other man, and Edward's drinking continued unchecked. Marshall's deep love of education persisted, but he couldn't keep his mind on his studies. His interest waned due to anger, depression, and lack of direction, which caused him to falter. He longed for success of some kind—any kind—but any available path of accomplishment bypassed his school and home life. All he witnessed were wayward brothers, alcoholic parents, and dead-end jobs. College was off-limits because of lack of funds and faltering grades. Nevertheless, Marshall refused to follow the same route as his brothers, and he wanted to escape from his parents and Youngstown.

I'm stuck here. Maybe a new environment will give me a new life. But where? How? Despite his earlier potential, he didn't possess the superhuman powers required to rise above his stifling environment. Lacking the drive to find another road to travel, Marshall drifted, waiting for an answer. He needed an intervention, something external that would lift him out of the morass from which he couldn't free himself.

CHAPTER FIVE

ONE GONE GI

In 1965, while Marshall languished in the rut of steel town, Ohio, a "little" war was underway in Vietnam. College students staged small and unreported protests until the U.S. started bombing in earnest. Still, protests were mostly held on and near college campuses, a physical and intellectual world away from Marshall.

He still held to the glamorized version of war depicted in Hollywood movies; through the silver screen, they beckoned him to serve his country and become a defender, too. Tired of being a nobody without worth, Marshall dreamed of becoming a champion, fighting evil, and transforming himself into a success, someone worthy of respect and admiration—someone he saw as totally opposite his parents. He believed he could use his hard-earned fighting skills to better himself and his future. He didn't yet realize the trouble his extra burden of anger would bring to his plans.

Marshall and his friend Judd walked past the Army recruiting office a few times and discussed the possibilities.

"What do you think, Judd?" Marshall asked.

"You know what, Brother? I think this is our ticket out of this crap hole. Man! I can fight for something real in the Army. I can make a name for myself outside of this town."

Marshall pledged his support, so together, they decided to join the Army as part of the buddy system, in, which the recruiter assured them, friends would be kept together through basic and advanced training.

Since Marshall was not yet eighteen, he had to get his parents' signatures on a release form. Remarkably (or maybe predictably), Ed and Ruthie consented with no questions or concerns. Marshall and his mother now shared a mutual respect, and she seemed surprised at his hurry to leave the family. On a day when the house was empty, his father at work, all the other children on their own or busy, and Ruthie off childcare duty for Eva's children, Marshall told his mother of his decision.

"Marshall, will you be okay?" she asked him. "I mean, what does this mean? Will you have to go to Vietnam?"

"Mom, I just want to be out of here. I can take care of myself. They will send me where they send me."

"You'll take all you've learned, right? I didn't raise no boy who can't take care of himself."

Don't I know that! Marshall recognized love in that comment and leaned in and gave his mom a warm hug as her lips trembled.

Once the recruitment forms were signed, Marshall quit school and prepared to leave home, the first time he would ever be away from his family. Even when roaming the streets, he always slept at home. Marshall, the first of his immediate and extended family, became a serviceman, and he wore pride on his chest. His MOS (Military Occupational Specialty), as assigned by his recruiter, was as a nuclear, biological, and chemical specialist (NBC) and ammunition specialist. He stood a bit taller when he thought of that specialty, and he hoped his parents' signatures would send him on a better, idyllic journey.

It's weird that they are the ones who must give permission to strike out on my own. I wish I could just go on with nobody's permission, Marshall thought. To him, they held him back all his life. He wanted complete freedom, not permission.

With two weeks to get his affairs in order, Marshall continued to spend time with Joyce, his current girlfriend. A classmate he'd met months before quitting school, they slept together right away. She didn't hide her pregnancy from Marshall, and going into the Army provided just the excuse he needed to back away from her. He didn't want the responsibility of fatherhood, and he sure didn't want to stay in Youngstown. Before he left, he told his mother about Joyce, and she took the news matter-of-factly.

Maybe she'll have to help; serves her right for the way she treated me. I just want out, Marshall thought with a bit of guilt, which he forgot as soon as he stepped into the recruiter's car for the journey to the military transport. As he left with no fanfare, he thought, *I'm gone. I'm out of here. I'm gone. Hallelujah!*

He had no clue about what he was walking into.

November 2, 1965, fifty-seven days after he turned seventeen, Marshall entered the service, proud to be an American serving his country. After no send-off from his family, the recruiter drove Marshall and his two friends Judd and Frank (who joined them when they told him their plans) to the Cleveland airport to board an Army-chartered commercial flight to the post where they would enter boot camp.

Post-flight and on the ground, an excited and nervous Marshall joined a large group of recruits on a deuce-and-a-half, a two-and-a-half-ton M35 cargo truck used to transport troops to Fort Jackson, named after President Andrew Jackson. Located near Columbia, South Carolina, Fort Jackson boasted one of the first Army installations to experience large-scale desegregation. Thousands of young men, both Black and White, went through basic at this 53,000-acre complex as they trained for the war in Vietnam. Marshall and his mates arrived at midnight, having spent the day in anxious anticipation of their next steps. As the bus rolled to a stop, Marshall caught the mirrored face of the smirking driver.

Uh oh.

He heard the whir and click of the doors, and a rush of cold air entered the bus, as did a red-faced, snarling drill instructor (DI). Marshall wasn't sure which boded worse, the chilly night air or the DI.

"Get up, slugs! Say hello to your new mama." He paused. "That would be me."

The recruits laughed and looked at each other, but only for a moment. With a voice that shook Marshall to his soul, the DI spewed expletives and spittle at the young men.

"Stop your laughing, idiots! I am not here to entertain you! Get your butts off the bus!" Propelled out of their seats, the new recruits disembarked and lined up facing the ordeal of orientation. The rest of the rigid, pithy DIs waited for them.

Marshall shuddered in the forty-degree temperature. He queued and waited with the rest of his fellow GIs. He shivered, and his stomach was far beyond butterflies; it did the jitterbug.

The unorganized chaos of the recruits as they tried to comply with the DI's shouts assaulted Marshall's sense of order. They had no idea how to line up. He fell into the jagged line on the wet ground, his shoes sinking into the mud as he faced a screaming, White DI whose face was as red as the Carolina clay Marshall saw on the ride over.

"Get moving! Do *not* stare at me, jerk water! Move your lazy butt to that section over there."

If Marshall expected an easy transition, this wasn't it. It didn't matter this man was White like the authority figures he recoiled from in the South; all that mattered was Marshall had better listen and obey.

"Yessir," Marshall said.

"Shut up! Did I tell you to speak?"

Marshall put his head down and followed his assigned orientation officer. The troops who stood in line settled in different companies based on their MOS. Faces and heads shaved at the processing center, they ate and proceeded to the general reception center to get some sack time.

As he fell asleep, Marshall realized the stark contrast to his upbringing. He embraced his first time apart from family. Instead of a shared rollaway bed, Marshall had his own mattress. Exhausted from stress and travel, the men collapsed into their bunks. The bickering he heard at home was replaced with snoring. He was good with that.

———

Whatever sleep Marshall got evaporated at 4 a.m. when the DI and his aides blasted into the barracks banging metal trashcans and dumping the recruits out of their beds. Marshall shook his head and rubbed his scratchy eyes and face.

Marshall marveled at their stamina. *Do these guys ever sleep?*

When he heard them arrive, he managed to rouse himself before his bunk was assaulted. Men unlucky enough to be upended plopped on the floor like buckets of wet rags. They were too tired to stiffen up for the barrage of discipline that followed, but they stood at attention as best they could.

Drill instructors are charged with educating individual recruits in everything it takes to be a member of the U.S. Army. They supervise all aspects of the training, discipline, competency, and physical and moral fitness of the troops. They are the first impression a soldier gets of the Army and the life in which he enlisted. They equip the recruits to fight and win regardless of their MOS. To say DIs are passionate about their profession is an understatement. It is not uncommon for a DI to spit blood from forceful recitation of orders.

Marshall stood at the end of his bunk, looked at his superior, and thought, *Does this man do anything but scream?*

"You are some nasty recruits," the DI said. "Make up your bunk so I can bounce a dime on it, get your clothes on, and get out into formation. You have three minutes."

Marshall blinked, dumbstruck. Then he rushed to follow the orders as the DI yelled, "Come on, maggots, move it! Maggots! You'd better move out of here. I can bust some heads if you don't move fast enough for me!"

That man sure likes bugs, Marshall thought as he high-stepped toward the door. He flew, and his feet skimmed the steps out of the building.

The discombobulated unit was out the door and in formation before sunlight could reach the camp.

The men lined up in formation and double-timed to supply to get their uniforms, boots, shirts, underwear, and the duffle bags to hold it all. Marshall gaped at his uniform with his name affixed to the left chest. The realization that he had a place to be somebody made him proud, and he temporarily forgot his screaming skull of a DI.

I'm here. I have a future. I can deal with these guys for eight weeks. I'm good.

The men were then trucked to their new home away from home for the duration, grouped by MOS in alphabetically ordered platoon barracks. Breakfast followed, and so began the routine of boot camp. Their quarters each featured two floors, double bunk beds, one large bathroom, and a working coal furnace. (Marshall double-checked.) Each man secured a footlocker where he placed all his bedding and belongings. After that first day of drills and physical training, Marshall fell into his bunk, bushed but happy to have his own space—a bunk, yes, but free from the abusive confines of home.

Marshall, like all the other men, double-timed (ran) everywhere. No matter what he did or where he went, he had to follow that routine. If anyone got caught doing less than that, the punishment was push-ups. Marshall understood consequences, and he always conformed during training.

Overall, Marshall loved boot camp once he got past the initial shock of DI hell. As he donned his uniform each morning, he felt like he embarked on a new journey. The future held unknowns for sure, but the newness of this current life suited him. The clear-cut orders and discipline propelled him, and he delighted in the structure of it all. Here he took the chance to learn and then succeed with the tools an Army education gave him. While he couldn't retain what his high school attempted to teach him because of the craziness of his life, he now grasped everything with newfound senses that had been dormant.

"Fall out for drill," the DI would say.

Cool, Marshall always thought. Each time, he fell out and got in his place, ready to march.

Hot or cold weather, he didn't mind. He tapped the soldier to his right to set his proper placement in the lineup. For Marshall, to march meant to dance—the cadence had a "soulishness" to it that made Marshall feel free. He always liked the soul music produced by Motown. The beats laid down by the likes of Stevie Wonder, The Temptations, and the Four Tops made him move with a rhythm that he felt to the depths of his soul. Marching to the meter of the DI's commands—*Left, left, left, right, left*—along with the troops' footfalls that sounded like deep clapping, made him recall the music he so loved. He moved as though dancing, but in time and pace with the other soldiers. He longed to do a cut and slide like James Brown, but he knew the DI would make him do fifty push-ups as penalty.

This is good. I can do this, Marshall thought again as he marched with joyful abandon. Some recruits struggled to find the rhythm of the march, and other guys would either get impatient with them or help them. Marshall helped; he liked seeing the perfection of the parade. Those who got angry did so because the march had to be repeated until the whole unit melded as one in time and on pace. The subjective eyes of the DI determined what perfection looked like, and if one guy couldn't get it down, no matter how much he tried, he *and* the unit had to do push-ups, the Army's disciplinary answer for almost any infraction.

Marshall learned how to do most everything the Army asked of him with confidence. He learned and thrived on the discipline and appreciated the value of being part of a team where each member entrusted his life to others. It was refreshing to him because of his dog-eat-dog fight for everything at home.

He learned to shoot a rifle, and when his DI said, "Hit it" (meaning, get to whatever he ordered), Marshall did it with no hesitation. The first lesson every recruit learns? Shut up and listen. Marshall knew how to do that from his premilitary orders and stripes at the hands of his mother. This time, however, he felt a greater purpose.

No matter what racial injustice was going on in the outside world, Marshall felt no discrimination at the hands of anyone in boot camp. He received the same treatment as all his fellow soldiers, both Black and White.

In the Army, squad leaders receive assignments over groups of four to ten soldiers, and Marshall's platoon possessed four squads. In basic, the squad leader position was usually a temporary one that lasted throughout their eight-week training. He reported directly to the DI, who chose them based on his perception of each recruit's skills.

Marshall's first squad leader bullied others and lacked basic people skills. Since Marshall had no patience for bullies, it didn't take long for them to butt heads. Marshall witnessed him make derogatory remarks to another recruit, and Marshall stood up for the ridiculed guy. He went straight up to the squad leader, nose to nose.

"You didn't have to treat him that way," Marshall said.

"Shut up, Brandon; get back in your place," said the squad leader.

"No, man, you were wrong to do that, and you at least owe him an apology."

The squad leader and Marshall faced off and were about to come to blows when another guy broke them up. The DI, who missed nothing, called Marshall into his office.

"Brandon, you think your squad leader has an easy job?" the DI said.

"I don't know if it's easy or not, Sir. I only know he shouldn't be so hateful with people."

The DI looked at Marshall for a moment and said, "Okay. You're going to be the squad leader from now on so you can see what it's like."

The DI promoted Marshall, and the former squad leader got stuck back in the ranks, compliant. Marshall treated his men well; he disciplined the men with fairness. They liked him and told him so.

"We want you to make it," many of them said to him.

Outside his high-school gang, this became the first time Marshall used his leadership abilities. In his new role—skills developed and honed—Marshall realized a true path to fulfilling his dream as a hero-soldier. He and the DI got along well once Marshall displayed his proficiencies and loyalty, and he served as squad leader through the end of basic training. Physical disciplines also went well for soldier Brandon. His unofficial fighter training in Youngstown prepared him for Army life in ways he never would have guessed. Hand-to-hand combat, marching, running, gunnery practice, and all the synchronized drills aided his fast-track toward excellent soldier life. He kept up and performed all his duties with ease. Even training in gas-filled rooms, where the men entered unmasked and put their protective gear on while in contaminated conditions, was easily mastered by Marshall.

Bring it on, he thought at every new challenge.

During the first two weeks of basic, the troops got nothing in the way of mail or phone calls. The men operated in submission mode; their focus had to be on the new environment and obedience to superiors. After that first two weeks, mail call came every day. Marshall found it difficult because he rarely received anything. As much as he wanted to be away from home, he still experienced disappointment when he watched others receive letters and packages, and nothing arrived for him.

Shoot, I'd even be happy to get something from Mom.

No one from home came to visit either while he underwent boot camp, but he was all right with that. Being away from the hometown madness was a balm to him, and he truly relished his newfound role as a soldier.

His mother did finally surprise him with a few short letters printed in her limited vocabulary. She updated him on news from home, just enough to let him know he was missed.

Marshall, in his naïveté and wonder, focused on his immediate surroundings and knew exactly what he had to do to excel at his new position as a squad leader to please his superiors. At home, he never knew when his mother would go off on him. Here, at least, orders came as regimented and clear. He saw guys wash out, not being able to meet the requirements of the Army, but in no way did Marshall plan to fail. He fought to make it, and he did everything ordered with no arguments, except when he saw mistreatment, as he had with his first squad leader.

He was so immersed in Army life and training that he had no idea what was happening in the world. He had no knowledge of the growing protests and news reports of the horrors of Vietnam. He would soon experience it firsthand.

———

After they completed basic training in December 1965, the men formally became soldiers at a graduation ceremony. Marshall was designated as an E2 (enlisted man private second class), the standard promotion when men complete basic training. No family or friends attended Marshall's graduation ceremony, but as he stood at attention, a wonderful realization hit him.

Hey! I graduated from something!

He received a thirty-day leave before scheduled to report to his next base, so Marshall took a Greyhound bus home to Youngstown. He relaxed and visited with friends and family, proud to show off his uniform. Despite what transpired as Marshall grew up in his home, his parents boasted and paraded their son around their friends. Perhaps they demonstrated vicarious pride; their son achieved something of note—something that would give him a greater freedom than they had yet to achieve. Marshall did not see his ex-girlfriend, Joyce, who had no place in his current plans and, he hoped, none in his future.

Marshall's friend Frank traveled with him to Youngstown and accompanied him to their next base. Marshall lost track of Judd, his other friend with whom he'd enlisted. Judd obtained an assignment to a different platoon in basic, breaking the Army promise of the buddy system. At that point, Marshall began to grieve relationships. He opened himself up to friendships, but mistrust better protected his heart from hurt. He learned not to give too much of himself to another person because he didn't want the sorrow of separation. Any day, a friend could get his orders to go elsewhere, and Marshall wouldn't know whether he'd ever see that person again.

In February 1966, Marshall and Frank reported to Fort McClellan, Alabama, for eight weeks of AIT (Advanced Individual Training) in each man's specific MOS. Having been born in Alabama, Marshall felt a little more at home, even though only a toddler when his family moved north. Fort McClellan was located in Calhoun County, only four counties away from Owens Cross Roads.

At Fort McClellan, Marshall became certified as a chemical decontamination specialist (CDS) as part of the Army's chemical corps. He spent a lot of time in classroom training, as well as the continuous rigorous physical and disciplinary training every soldier experiences. Marshall did well in the classroom setting; he had the gift of an almost photographic memory. Stringent training and Marshall's intuitive smarts allowed him to test well for the position and then excel at it.

His CDS education included how to react and assist in the case of radiation fallout from a bomb or other incendiary device. He grasped all a soldier needed to know about it, including its kill zone and rate. The kill zone is the area directly affected by a detonated incendiary device, be it yards or even miles. The kill rate is how many people will die because of the bomb or other device being detonated. Marshall joined other CDS trainees as they learned how to mix the flammable material used in flamethrowers, in addition to all the other agents he might have to produce, administer, or clean up during deployments.

Because he worked with such things, Marshall received top-secret clearance. The biological warfare agents Marshall processed included napalm, Agent Orange, and tear gas, as well as live nerve and blister agents, such as mustard gas. At that time, Agent Orange and napalm were used extensively in Southeast Asia. These chemical agents and biological warfare caused a furor during and after the war in Vietnam. Soldiers shared stories of how they lifted napalm-attack victims and saw the victims' flesh peel away from their bones. But soldier Brandon did his job to the best of his abilities, ignorant of the short- and long-term effects of the chemicals he mixed and administered during the war in Vietnam. During his tenure at CDS school, Marshall worked a five-day week and had the weekends off. He took the opportunity to visit his maternal Aunt Bessie in Huntsville, with whom he always had a peaceful relationship. She fed him well and let him get good rest, and after a weekend there, he would take the bus back to base.

Marshall's buddy Frank, still stationed in the same unit with him, talked Marshall into a trip to Birmingham to see the sights and maybe find some girls. Frank and Marshall were approached by a couple of guys who ended up stinging Frank with a scam called a *pigeon drop.*

One guy approached Frank. "Hey, man," he said. "Where's that blues club? It's supposed to be around here somewhere."

Frank said, "I don't know. We just got into town."

Marshall's keen distrust for people made him hang back and watch the scene unfold. Another guy came up to Frank and said, "Hey! I just found an envelope full of money over there! You guys see anyone lose this thing?" He showed Frank the envelope.

Frank whistled a long note. "Dang, that looks like a lot of money."

The guy said, as he looked at Frank and Marshall, "Will you guys hang on to this while I look for who might have lost it? I'll find a cop too."

He started off but stopped and asked, "Um, how do I know you guys won't take off with the money?"

Frank just shrugged his shoulders.

"Tell you what," the guy said, "you give me $50, so I know you won't take off." Frank thought of the money in that envelope, copped a glance at Marshall, and said,

"Sure." He and the other bystander forked over $50 cash.

"Okay, I'm gonna look for the guy and find the cops too."

After a few minutes, the guy who asked for directions said, "I'd better go see if I can find the guy." He looked up and said, "There he goes," and he took off after him.

Neither guy returned.

Frank said, "Man! Marshall, we got ourselves some free money!"

He opened the envelope, found torn strips of newspaper, and uttered every expletive Marshall had ever heard, and some new ones.

Frank was had, and so was Marshall, because he ended up paying for the hotel room that night. When wearing their uniforms, soldiers were generally well treated, but in their constant search for obliging women in less-than-savory parts of town, they were targets for scam artists. From then on, Marshall and Frank learned to recognize cons and got out of the area where they sensed one was about to go down. Marshall kept his money in his sock and his internal radar on alert.

Frank was a dark Black man and very nice. His trusting demeanor proved his undoing, however, when targeted by a sting. A good singer, Frank won a few talent shows while on base. A few years older than Marshall, Frank also smoked cigarettes and drank, often to excess. The only time Marshall got drunk, Frank stood up for him when another guy punched Marshall so hard he blackened both eyes. Marshall swore he'd never get that drunk again because it rendered him defenseless.

After eight weeks of training, the Army promoted Marshall to PFC (private first class).

Usually, after one year of service, a private will be automatically promoted to PFC rank, but Marshall, on his merit, rose after a few months. His rank still meant subservience to the CO (Commanding Officer), and from there, a soldier could be promoted to specialist or corporal. For the moment, Marshall enjoyed his new rank. He then received orders to report to Edgewood Arsenal, along the I-95 corridor north of Baltimore, Maryland. There he trained further in chemical specialties. His buddy Frank got orders for somewhere else, and Marshall lost track of him.

Edgewood Arsenal formed part of a research establishment that sat in a secluded section of the suburbs. While there, Marshall continued enhancing his skills, working with all aspects of biological and chemical warfare. His duty included him in a "what if" team.

What if the troops were hit with nerve gas?

What if the enemy used biological agents on the soldiers or even within the U.S.?

Since he knew how to mix napalm and other herbicides and nerve gasses, he also learned how to clean them up in the event of any offensive scenario against the U.S. or its troops. He sprayed the agents and burned things up as part of his training. Mixing the agents into different consistencies developed a different chemical, and he had to know how to sanitize that too. Marshall also became proficient at operating a flamethrower, which he enjoyed. As he trained with one, he pictured an evil opponent incinerated by fire.

Marshall's elite company accompanied the delivery any time chemical warfare components went to a war zone. As the components were readied and transported to their departure point within the United States, members of his troop personally oversaw the shipment. Many such items traversed heavily populated areas along the East Coast. As a CDS, Marshall often went along after his company leader alerted local authorities about the shipment.

When not on assignment for chemical duty, Marshall served as driver for the post commanding "full-bird" colonel, so-called because of the silver eagle insignia placed on the left side of his uniform cap. Marshall shined up the staff car and drove him all over the Washington, D.C., vicinity. Marshall's duties also included picking up dignitaries from the airport and chauffeuring them to various spots in the Capitol area. Many times, he had no idea where his destination lay, so he learned the area as he drove those guys around.

Marshall's dad bought a '59 Chevy while Marshall lived at home but never drove it. Marshall was the only one who did, and he learned to drive running errands for his mom and going to school. Those skills helped him as he drove for the colonel. He loved navigating the D.C. area because it was so vast compared to what seemed a much smaller Youngstown. He embraced a sense of freedom and adventure.

On July 28, 1966, while Marshall served at Edgewood, Joyce gave birth to his son, Keith. Marshall, a deadbeat dad, refused to participate. Ruthie, however, helped care for Keith and babysat him. Marshall thought she loved on him better than she loved on her own children. Sometimes she watched the boy for a week at a time. Marshall, in the meantime, had moved on to his next female conquest-of-the-month.

CHAPTER SIX

"YOU GOTTA DO YOURS NOW"

The war in Vietnam escalated, and toward the end of 1966, President Johnson increased the troop count to close to 400,000 men. In June, Marshall's unit received orders to deploy to Vietnam, but Marshall hadn't broken the age barrier. No soldier could go into battle under the age of eighteen, and Marshall had three months until he gained his right to fight. His orders retracted, he continued with regular duties until his birthday. Once eighteen, he received his orders and a thirty-day leave before he shipped out to Vietnam.

Marshall arrived home in his PFC uniform, once again proud to be part of something bigger than himself and his family. His parents busied themselves, inviting friends over to show off their son. As Marshall's departure date drew near, the revelry lessened, and the gravity of the situation hit them all. There loomed a real chance he might not come home. Marshall cried, his sister wept, and his mother sobbed louder than the rest. His father was not around when Marshall left. In almost direct comparison with his father not being there for him (physically or morally), Marshall did not visit Joyce or his new son.

Ruthie's emotional state kept her home, so Eva took her brother to the small airstrip in Youngstown, where he boarded a commercial flight to Oakland, California. The Oakland Army Base at that time contained the largest military port complex in the world, and it engulfed a sea of servicemen. Marshall spent a few days processing and traveled to Vietnam as an independent in another unit. He felt detached; he trusted his old unit, and now he had to try to fit in with a new one. Plus, he held the only top-secret clearance in his new unit. He withdrew more into himself as his trust-no-one instinct sharpened.

As the troops boarded the C-141, Starlifter, to Wake Island in the Philippines to refuel, Marshall kept his mouth shut and blended in with the herd. In spring 1963, President Kennedy had ceremonially pushed a button to open the Georgia hanger doors and introduce the troop- and cargo-moving workhorse. The Starlifter, so named as the result of a winning contest entry, transported myriad soldiers in the sixties.

The men settled onto canvas jump seats with tasteless box lunches for the nine-hour flight. The meager meal provided little sustenance, but the anxious men found it hard to eat anyway. With no room to move about, Marshall felt debilitated by the cacophony of the engines and men's shouts as they tried to surmount the noise. He tried to rest, but with no room to stretch out, he pondered what lay ahead. He thought of his friends from basic and looked around at the strangers near him. Seeing his old unit ship out ahead of him was one thing; being amid unknown servicemen made him regret the loss of his trusted buddies even more.

A soldier develops bonds that start in basic training. These bonds form the necessary allegiance that builds trust in fellow soldiers; they learn to count on each other and are willing to give their lives for these buddies. Marshall felt abandoned, which reminded him of his father's desertion. At that moment, loneliness overshadowed his drive to be a hero and serve his country well.

Marshall strained to see if any other bubbas were on the plane. He'd have to scream to make himself heard over the roar of the engines if he saw anyone else matching his Black skin, so he lowered his head, as did most of the other soldiers. Some of the men stared blankly ahead, as if they could see through the enormous piles of duffle bags and assorted equipment. The plane looked like a workhorse, and nearly two hundred soldiers jockeyed for elbow room and a comfortable position. All Marshall saw was a confused mass of Army-green duffels, their color dulled by the windowless cavern. He could hear only the deafening motors and smell only his fear. After the stop at Wake, the plane once again headed toward Vietnam.

The landing and takeoff did nothing to calm his nerves, and Marshall experienced increased misgivings about what awaited him in Vietnam. It served him right to doubt.

Finally, the engine's drone lulled Marshall into a light sleep until he was jolted awake at the sound of the landing gear as it locked into place. His mouth and eyes were dry, and he had to use the head, but the plane was on final approach, so no one had permission to get out of his seat. He entered Vietnam airspace as tired as he'd ever been.

Great way to start my tour. He muttered an appropriate expletive under his breath. Jostled by wheels down, the men sat up, rubbed their heads, wiped the drool off their chins, and stretched.

On November 2, 1966, Marshall's new unit landed in the Ia Drang Valley (Pleiku) in the central highlands of Vietnam, where permanent runways were not feasible. Instead, they landed on portable, pierced-steel planking (Marston Mats, or M8A1s) built by the Army's Corps of Engineers. Almost a year-to-the-day previous, a fierce battle took place on the spot where Marshall and his fellow soldiers landed. The 1st Battalion, 7th Air Cavalry, led by Lt. Col. Harold Moore, lost over two hundred men. The battle gained distinction as dramatized in the book *We Were Soldiers* Once . . . *and Young* by Harold G. Moore and Joseph L. Galloway. Thankfully, Marshall wasn't aware of that battle. This landing was at a safe landing zone (LZ) secured by the infantry.

Marshall carried not only his Army gear and gun but also his street smarts, his love of order and fair treatment, and the fury left over from years of abuse. He stepped into a war that would include the horrors of combat, the pervasiveness of drugs, and the reality of racism.

Despite a job well done in basic and specialist training, Marshall walked into war as a raging man, brooding and scared of what lay ahead but with emotional fists up, ready for any fight that came at him or that he could start.

Blast furnace heat struck him when he walked onto the gangway. He forgot all about his need to relieve himself.

Marshall looked at the guy next to him and said, "What the hell is this?"

His fellow GI shrugged his shoulders. "I don't know, man," he said. "How do these people live in this?"

"And what's that smell?" Marshall wanted to cover his nose, but he held all his gear, and his hands weren't free.

The odor of a damp, almost 100 percent humidity atmosphere mixed with the jet fuel and soldier sweat. Added to that were the smells of the dung-fueled fires that heated local cook pots and the urine and feces from locals lacking even basic sanitation.

Marshall strained to sniff his armpits to make sure the smell wasn't him. His knees nearly buckled from the stench as he stood at the door of the plane.

"Marshall," said the other GI, "get moving. The sergeant is glaring at you."

Marshall didn't realize he had stopped. His fear almost paralyzed him, but he forced himself to walk on, and he followed the soldier in front of him. He looked up and squinted at the harsh sunlight. *The sun never shines this hot at home.*

Marshall thought about his father and how he berated him nonstop as he grew up. His words stung Marshall even now. "Y'all will never be nothin." "You'll never amount to anything."

As he exhumed those shallow buried memories, he thought, *I will not get back on that plane, much as I want to. I will not get on a plane out of here until I have completed my tour. My family needs to know I can do this and do it well. I will not fail, and they will all be proud of me.*

With that resolve, he called to his fellows, "Hold up, I'm coming."

Marshall already experienced the first thing most soldiers remember about arriving in-country—the smell. As he looked around, he saw nothing but jungle and breathed in nothing but stink. The U.S. Army started the napalm and Agent Orange assault in 1965, plenty of time for its tang to permeate the air and provide a nasty olfactory welcome to newly deployed soldiers. In addition, the odors of monkeys, strange trees, and grasses added to the mix. To Marshall, nowhere else now smelled as sweet as home, even if home smelled of sooty steel mills.

Despite this double dose of nastiness, he planned to take his chances and fight the war in Vietnam. He was a proud soldier and got caught up in his identification as one. As he walked wide-eyed into the theater of war, he asked himself, *How does this work?*

As young, scared, and naïve Marshall joined his brothers-in-arms on the tarmac, a group of soldiers waited to board. They pushed past Marshall's unit as if stepping out of the dark underbelly of the spiritual realm. They lifted their bags as they walked by, now set for home after their tour of duty in what the soldiers called "the Nam."

The soldiers en route back home continued to pass him as they headed for the transport plane. Marshall experienced his first glimpse of the "thousand-yard stare," a look worn by battle-weary soldiers whose escape from the shock of war is revealed in eyes that seem to stare a thousand yards out, unfocused. The windows to their souls looked dark and empty, but one spoke as he walked by Marshall, "I done did mine; you gotta do yours now." What Marshall would soon call his camping trip to the middle of nowhere freaked him out.

Marshall saw only tents—no permanent structures. Another soldier who had some rank instructed the men where to go and assigned them to their specific tents. These temporary accommodations housed fifty guys each. The tents had no solid bathroom facilities, only a tube pushed into the ground for urinating, and makeshift outhouses. There was no hope for hot water or conveniences of that sort; it was a tropical jungle—it sweltered.

The Vietnamese language also assaulted Marshall's senses. The local villagers did menial duties around the American camps and shouted to each other and to the soldiers as Marshall watched. The sound was harsh to his ears as he heard them try to speak to the soldiers in their native language, which the men could not understand. He felt he'd arrived on Mars without anyone to tell him what to expect. Marshall relied on his COs and fellow soldiers for direction.

Marshall and the unit stayed in the temporary quarters at Pleiku for three days while being processed for in-country duty. Afterward, he shipped to Cam Ranh Bay for three months, assigned to an ordnance company whose responsibility included handling and distribution of arms and ammo to the infantrymen. Marshall sensed safety at heavily fortified Cam Ranh Bay, a major supply spot for the war away from the primary battle lines. The soldiers called it "the sandbox" because of its many beaches. They used elevated boardwalks to get around most of the base. Marshall had never seen such beautiful, blue water. He wished he had time to explore it more.

Marshall lodged in a hooch, a medium-sized hut that held about thirty men. With a wooden frame and tin roof, it sat on a concrete pad and had screens for walls and privacy partitions that reached three-quarters of the way to the ceiling. Hooch girls (native Vietnamese), whom the soldiers called *mama sans*, served as house servants. They earned two to three dollars a week. The women cleaned the dwelling as well as the soldiers' boots and clothing.

Marshall met lots of new people, and on his third day, he fell in with a guy named Dale, who slept in the same hooch. Marshall knew him from his chemical corps training in Alabama. Dale was a native Virginian, a light-skinned Black man with large eyes. He and Marshall shared the same MOS, and both were moved from chemical specialty to ordnance when they got shipped to the Nam. Marshall delighted to find someone he already knew, so when Dale and some other guys took Marshall up on a nearby hill to "show him something," he readily followed.

That "something" changed his life.

"Hey, man, you want to go with me?" Dale asked Marshall. "I want to turn you on to something."

"Yeah, man, what you got?" Marshall looked for diversions wherever they showed up.

Six guys made their way up to an isolated spot atop a nearby sand dune, out of the way of official eyes, ears, and noses. When they arrived at the crest, they all sat down in a circle. One of the guys started filling a pipe.

Wow, man, I never smoked tobacco out of a pipe, Marshall thought, *but what's so interesting about that?* He'd smoked cigarettes since he was twelve. He snatched them from his mom's and sister's stashes. *Maybe this gets a better buzz.* In his heart, he suspected it was weed. Once verified, he hesitated because he always believed marijuana to be evil, like heroin. The guys who'd already started smoking laughed at everything, and Marshall couldn't pass up the chance to have a good time.

One guy filled the pipe, lit it, and passed it to the next guy, and Marshall learned as he watched. When it got to him, he took a huge toke and held it in.

This is weed. Don't cough. Don't cough.

The bowl didn't empty until after three times around. Since it was Marshall's first time and the weed was potent, he had no clue what to expect. His cocky self didn't back down.

He was toast—burnt toast.

Somehow, he managed to get back to his hooch and fell asleep on his cot until reveille the next morning.

That he had no hangover was a huge plus to Marshall. Yet, he felt hollow-headed.

Next time, fool, don't smoke as much.

He gave himself permission to smoke, but not so much that it incapacitated him. Weed could be had cheap and easy from the many "shop keepers" in the villages.

From that day on, Marshall smoked, along with many of the other guys, and got high every day. Some guys drank beer, some drank heavier alcohol, some smoked weed, and some moved on to hard drugs like opium and heroin. Everyone did something to relieve either their pain (both physical and mental) or boredom or to calm their fears. Marshall simply liked it.

One day while off duty and high, Marshall sat in the shade and watched a fellow bubba get berated by a superior. Later he asked him, "What were you doing wrong?"

"Man," the soldier said, "I don't know, but that son of a witch's mother busted me and revoked my pass into town."

"That's not right," Marshall mused, more to himself than to the other soldier.

The guy closest to him in the unit's hooch received lots of magazines from home, and he let Marshall have them after he finished. Reading them, Marshall faced his naïveté when he found out that from 1965–67, the death rate for Blacks killed in Nam was greater than 20 percent, while they made up but eleven percent of the US population. He learned about the riots in Newark, New Jersey, and Detroit in the summer of 1967.

As he descended further into the grasp of his daily highs, and as he saw the inhumanity and injustice of many of his superiors, his innocence turned to cynicism, and smoking dope became a shield. The weed gave Marshall courage and protection and a bit of stupidity. He couldn't tell the difference at that point; it was simply how he functioned. Less than a month after he arrived, some of the guys encouraged him to fraternize with the local females who lived near the base camp. The girls often openly advertised their availability to the men. Marshall was no prude; he'd already had plenty of sex at his young age.

The normal procedure was to put in for a pass to go to the village; they were rarely refused. The camp had barbed-wire fences and plenty of guards to keep the enemy out, but the safety measures also obstructed the men's libidos. They were a long way from home and were game for some fun.

Late one evening, the other guys egged Marshall on and told him how to get out of camp and into the village without a pass. Not being one to refuse the companionship of a lady (even a lady of the night), Marshall accompanied the men who headed into the village that evening. A few of them jumped the fence and ran. Marshall started to gingerly climb over the barbed-wire fence after the others were out of sight. He had just dropped to the other side when he heard,

"Halt! Halt!"

He ran toward the village and didn't know where to go. When he arrived, he thought maybe the MPs (military policemen) had given up the chase. No such luck. When he couldn't find the girls, he headed back toward the base; and an MP chased him down. Once he caught up to Marshall, who ran at half speed, he drove him to his knees and put a .45 to his head.

"Take it easy, man," Marshall said.

The MP cocked his pistol.

"Hold up. Hold up, man," Marshall said.

———

Marshall, at Cam Ranh Bay less than a month, was arrested and put into the base stockade. His first sergeant got him out and took him to the CO's office the next morning.

"What were you doing?" the CO said.

"There are girls in the village, and I wanted to go see them," Marshall said. "Look, Brandon," the CO said, "you don't have to do that. If you're feeling that way, come see me, and I'll give you a pass."

Marshall saw quite a bit of that CO while stationed at Cam Ranh Bay; he got passes every chance he could. Marshall thought the Vietnamese women were beautiful, and he couldn't resist when one said, "I love you too much, GI."

However, Marshall did not escape punishment for that first infraction. He received an Article 15, dispensed for minor infractions at the discretion of the CO. Article 15s and other reprimands could either be steps toward a court-martial or could stop with a one-time punishment. He received ten days' extra duty cleaning up around the base. What became a temporary job to him was twelve hours on and twelve hours off. He also garnered a fine of twenty-five dollars and company-area restriction for the duration. His daily regimen of company drills and duties was not lessened while he served his punishment.

Marshall enjoyed being a good fighter when he roamed the streets of Youngstown, his self-professed meritorious activity. His proclivity for fighting followed him into the service, and he bolstered it with indoctrination into political/societal savvy. Civil rights news from home introduced Marshall to the writings of Eldridge Cleaver, Malcolm X, Martin Luther King Jr., and the like.

As a teenager, he grieved along with most other Black Americans when JFK was assassinated because they saw the president as favorable toward them. However, teenage Marshall was more concerned about his own little world and not thoroughly informed on the rising Civil Rights Movement at the time. A bit older, when Malcolm X was murdered in February 1965, Marshall lamented his death as an act certain to retard elevation of the status of the Black man in America. His civil-rights education intensified while in Nam, and when Martin Luther King Jr. was murdered in April 1968, Marshall reeled from the news.

Marshall strode around the base as if on a mission to stand for all Black men everywhere, no matter who got in his way. The combination of his fighting instincts and his growing Black pride was volatile.

He'd fight for any reason that suited him. If a guy looked at him with what he considered disdain, Marshall hit him. Marshall was no longer afraid to start a fight; he felt the fight had already started when he believed he was dissed in any way. The other soldiers knew he would make a stand for others, but he stood mostly for himself. He had a reputation with the men, and, one by one, anyone who wanted to build his own status off Marshall's backed away. Though a fighter, Marshall had always been sensitive to how others were treated, and now he became even touchier about treatment received by his Black brothers and sisters. He noticed how Black soldier-brothers received the brunt of crap duty and were often placed in harm's way, far out of proportion to White soldiers. He stewed, and, as he consciously watched the injustice, he steamed.

As if he needed another instigator, Hanoi Hannah stoked his ire. She was a radio broadcaster on a Vietnamese station the guys listened to. Three times a day, she broadcast entertainment and propaganda for the Communist North Vietnamese government. Her mission? To demoralize US servicemen under the guise of pleasurable diversions. She highlighted the plight of the Black man by reporting on the race riots and one time said, "Go home, Black man. Your war is not in Vietnam; it's in America."

Marshall thought, *She's right.*

Marshall's superiors did not take kindly to his fighting or the way he spoke up when he saw others mishandled and mistreated by their cohorts. He became the unofficial spokesperson of the Black soldiers in his platoon, and his commanders finally addressed his fighting.

"Okay, Brandon," they said, "you want to fight? We are going to send you up north; they need fighters up there."

His three months at Cam Ranh Bay were fruitful for Marshall because he gained street cred with other soldiers, both for his pugilism and his protection of weaker brothers. Since his commanding officers didn't see it that way, they sent him to An Khê for the remainder of his time in country. Dale remained in Cam Ranh Bay, and they lost touch for the rest of Marshall's time in Nam. But a resourceful Marshall never lost contact with weed suppliers.

An Khê is typical of much of Vietnam; it lies within the mountainous region that dominates the northern two-thirds of the country. The Army had cleared such a large area at its Camp Radcliff base to handle the constant movement of helicopters the soldiers nicknamed it the "golf course." Lush tropical forests surrounded the base camp in An Khê, forests that hid the movements of the North Vietnamese army. Troops saw constant action there, and Commanding General Westmoreland considered Radcliff a base of great strategic importance because of its proximity to Laos. Marines reinforced the area due to the belief that Vietnamese forces were increasing in that remote area.

I'm not in Kansas anymore, Marshall thought when he arrived and noticed the massive infantry and air movement at the base. It was less than two hours away from Cam Ranh Bay but seemed more like a repulsive netherworld.

Once again assigned to a new unit, he went directly to the personnel office upon arrival, and someone asked him, "What are you doing here?"

Not understanding their question, he stood at attention and voiced no reply. Then it hit him. His former CO was in such a hurry to get him out of Cam Ranh Bay, he shipped Marshall with no orders. If that officer had been in front of him, Marshall would have decked him.

At Cam Rahn Bay, his duty lay with the First Logistical Ordnance, and Marshall witnessed perimeter bombing (bombs dropped just outside the area held by the U.S. and South Vietnamese army). He also saw action by the First Air Cavalry as their raids hit portions of the Ho Chi Minh Trail in Laos. The elite First Air Cav. made the first widespread use of helicopters in the war.

When Marshall arrived at An Khê—especially being shipped without orders—he felt mishandled. He endured meeting a whole new set of people, and by that time, he had become so immersed in his role as a Black man under siege by his superiors that his instincts for injustice sharpened even more. On constant lookout for any mistreatment of his Black brothers, he grew angrier each day. Marshall heard about the US protests from soldiers just arriving from the States, and he read news reports of civil unrest all over America. He went half-crazy from what he knew happened to Blacks both at home and at his base.

The first sergeant at An Khê gave Marshall work only dispensed to Black soldiers, like twelve-hour KP duty ("kitchen police," where men are responsible for preparation, setup, and cleanup of food and mess hall implements). Coupled with the heat, KP made twelve hours feel like sixteen. He'd arise at five a.m. and head straight to duty. He didn't get relieved until six or seven that evening. As he understood it, the KP-duty schedule rotated once a month with other men. His new superiors made him do KP at least twice a month. He observed the first sergeant showing favoritism to other men—White men. The superiors exempted White soldiers from such long duties, while Marshall and the other Black soldiers regularly received those assignments. Marshall maintained his flamethrower attitude and went to the first sergeant with his grievances.

"Man, you made me do that duty more than once. I'm doing work I'm not supposed to be doing. I'm supposed to be doing ordnance duties," Marshall said as he stood close to the sergeant.

"I'm sorry. I made a mistake," the sergeant said as he barely looked up from his desk.

Marshall's patience evaporated. "You make another mistake like that, and I'll kill you." The first sergeant reported Marshall's threat to the CO, who called Marshall into his office. Both were White, and they were waiting for Marshall.

Oh, man. Here we go again, White men lording it over me.

Marshall stood at attention before them. He was shocked when all he got was a reprimand and an order to get back to work and stop causing trouble.

Marshall thought about fragging the first sergeant. (Fragging is military slang for the killing of an unpopular superior, often with a grenade.) Marshall didn't care if everyone else liked the guy; he didn't. At that time and place, a lot of frag incidents occurred using antipersonnel weaponry. The practice increased as the war dragged on, and morale and discipline decreased. Marshall harbored disgust fueled by the treatment he received but also by the conditions that drove Americans to kill their own countrymen. Fragging happened more than it was reported, and it had already happened in Marshall's unit.

In his anger, Marshall started confronting people other than his sergeant, and his intimidation included more threats to kill. With his reputation, other guys shied away from him; and he became a loner, an introvert with thoughts that rarely morphed into anything good. Being in ordnance gave him access to everything he needed to carry out even his most deadly threats—ammo, antipersonnel mines, and grenades.

The hard meanness Marshall carried with him into war mutated into an impenetrable fortress, and he considered himself a killer. He knew he could kill if pushed too hard. Oddly enough, when he finally came close to following through, something made him stop short. His thoughts of fragging the first sergeant were immediately followed by another rationalization. *Man, what am I thinking? I can't do that . . . can I?* He still had a sense of right and wrong, no matter how much the daily dose of weed dulled his perceptions.

Marshall was constantly tired and high, so no matter what he did, he couldn't relax. The stink of the country turned into the stink of racism, and Marshall was constantly enraged, always on edge.

One day after another long stretch of KP, Marshall went to the enlisted men's club to try to unwind. Some Filipino girls came into the club and entertained the men by dancing to Motown hits. The guys in front of Marshall were standing, and he couldn't see the show, so he stood. The guys behind Marshall poked him in the back and told him to sit down. He remained standing. They poked him again, harder. Marshall unloaded his baggage of racism-fueled hate. The White guy who stuck his finger into his back was an easy target for what happened next.

Marshall punched one of the guys hard. He fought with such vehemence that he lost his watch. They turned the place out like a television saloon brawl. Marshall split before any MPs came. He felt justified to put the hurt on some White guys and get away with it.

———

Marshall's company did what is called "ammo-humping." They supervised and delivered the ammunition used by the infantry. Once conveyed to Marshall's unit, the men stored the ammo in magazine bunkers. (A magazine is a storage device for bullets used in a gun and is either a separate component or part of the gun itself.) When the ammo initially came in, Marshall's unit sorted it, organized it, and ticketed it. They filled all the infantry requests and used forklifts to move the supplies around. With no forklift (which sometimes happened), the men had to load the ammo by hand in temperatures that hovered between 115 and 120 degrees. Marshall envisioned slaves at work in a cotton field, and he again spoke his mind to the CO.

"It's not right that you have all of us Black guys in the field, and you White guys are in this cool office."

The CO took his time and answered as he smirked. "Brandon," he said.

Marshall cursed as he answered. (It was considered okay to swear at a superior as long as "Sir" was attached to the epithet.) "I don't want to hear any more from you," the CO said. "You need to go up to this place called Bồng So'n. They need you up there."

Bồng So'n sat northeast of An Khê, even closer to Laos. It was the site of a battle, January 28—February 12, 1966, again involving Lt. Col. Hal Moore's forces against two battalions of the North Vietnamese army. The U.S. and South Vietnamese armies recorded a limited victory, because the NVA (North Vietnamese army) burrowed itself into nearby mountains and forests, which made them hard as a tick to dislodge. Still, the U.S. forces inflicted damage on the North Vietnamese army, and the locals' suspicion of the U.S.-led troops grew. Marshall knew about the battle and his enthusiasm to follow orders waned.

By then, Marshall was "short." His time left to serve in Nam stood at about two months—sixty-one days, 1464 hours—and he counted every minute. When a soldier's time gets short, he becomes even more careful, not wanting anything to ruin his chance to go home. Looking the wrong way or stepping in the wrong place could mean death. No, Marshall wanted nothing to do with Bồng So'n.

"They don't need me up there," Marshall said.

His CO reacted. "Go up there; you'll get a promotion."

"I don't need no promotion. I don't want to go up there. I want to go home," Marshall fumed.

"You will go where I order you to go, Brandon."

Marshall spewed an ugly curse at the CO and quickly added, "Sir."

The CO acted on his promise, and less than a day later, Marshall found himself at the outpost LZ for helicopters called Bồng So'n. He thought it crazy. Marshall looked around at the mayhem—the guys firing artillery—and it didn't look or feel secure. He reported to the CO. Marshall thought he looked like a cowboy, a gun-toting, black-hat-wearing cowboy.

The word about Marshall being a fighter who resisted White authority preceded him.

As he stood and awaited his assignment, the CO slammed his desk with his fists.

You ain't impressing me, buddy, Marshall thought.

The CO took out his sidearm and leveled it at Marshall's face. They locked eyes. The CO affected a David Janssen grin, one side of his mouth cocked higher than the other. Marshall's feet sweat in his boots, and he couldn't move. He glanced toward the door; the shadow of a guard blocked his escape.

Nowhere to run. Dang. Will this cloud shoot me? (*Cloud* was a derogatory term Blacks used for Whites.)

The CO tilted his head, twisted his wrist, and shot the gun at the floor near Marshall's feet. Marshall flinched and squeezed his hands into fists, but he did not jump.

Okay, fool, I may not be able to raise my gun at you, but I know karate and can put some moves on you if you try that again, Marshall thought as he inched backward.

"Ahh, got that rat," the CO said as he returned his gun to the desk. He smiled as if he had scored a triumph.

Marshall still wasn't buying the act. He knew he'd been part of a cat-and-mouse game the CO was playing with him. And the CO wasn't through.

"I heard about how you guys are smoking."

While true, Marshall had just arrived at this outpost, so the CO's remark confirmed his suspicion that word about him preceded his appearance.

"No, sir," Marshall lied as the CO told him to get out of his office.

His former CO tried to catch the guys from Marshall's tent as they smoked weed. He held surprise raids, but in the short time Marshall spent in his command, he failed. Marshall kept his stash hidden in some sandbags and never got caught. Instead, his superior used another tactic to try to suppress Marshall; he sent him to this different, more dangerous outpost.

Even during his rebellion and continuous weed-induced haze, Marshall remained good at his job operating the forklift that unloaded convoy supplies. The Bồng Sơn CO sent Marshall to LZ English, a firebase further north. (A firebase is a temporary outpost that supplies artillery coverage outside the perimeter of a more permanent base.) LZ English was the base of the 173rd Airborne Brigade. It lay right next to what the soldiers called Sniper's Village, so named because the VC (Viet Cong) snipers came out at night.

As Marshall arrived, sustained incoming fire lit up LZ English. Mortars screamed in, and the ground shook from the thunder of the 155-mm artillery shells being fired in response. Marshall didn't know if the bombing came from the US or the enemy, and he ducked for cover wherever the officers ordered him. Marshall spent about six weeks there, supplying ordnance to the soldiers.

Whether because of his last commander at Bồng Sơn, he didn't know, but the CO of LZ English decided to send Marshall to an even more dangerous outpost. The road that led to it was mainly mud and huge, bone-jarring potholes with many cows along the wayside. As he rumbled along in a slow-moving forklift, cursing the CO, Marshall felt his anxiety and anger rise. Marshall lumbered through a village on the way up, drawing not a few looks from the locals.

He grumbled to himself as he put on his dog for no one in particular, just as a display of his mood. (A Black man showing his mettle was called putting on his "dog.")

White man trying to put me down, again.

When Marshall arrived, that base too exploded under rocket fire. Mortar rounds tore in and when he stopped the forklift, the guys at the base stared at him like he had just stepped off an alien ship.

"Man, where *is* your escort?" they said.

"Was I supposed to have an escort?"

Marshall was through; he done did his. Ready to get out of that hole, he started to turn around. He didn't report to the CO; he rotated the forklift and started back down the road. He didn't even look to see if he had enough diesel for the thirty-mile trek back to LZ English.

The guys objected, "Man, you got to wait for an escort."

"No, man, I got to didi." (*Didi* was slang for leaving—fast!) He lit out on the large contraption, his trip back taking place in the waning daylight when the VC came out of hiding. The village locals weren't so benign as on his way up. As he drove back, they were seething, emboldened by the sure arrival of the VC, who would get this Black man out of their environment. They came out in force, throwing rocks and spitting at him. Marshall didn't see any VC yet. Nevertheless, he stepped on the gas pedal and tried to make the forklift go faster than its top speed of eight miles an hour. He grimaced with clenched teeth and a clenched butt.

Lord, get me out of here!

Somehow, by luck or divine intervention, Marshall made it safely back to the firebase.

The first thing he wanted to do as he shut down the machine was to throw a grenade into the CO's office. On his way, something again stopped him—he didn't know what, but he knew it was not for him to do.

For the remainder of his six weeks there, he kept his nose down and made no waves. No way he wanted to get sent back to that outpost.

Then Marshall saw the bodies.

He hadn't fired his weapon while in-country and never saw the killing close-up, but he witnessed the aftereffects. Marshall saw the storage and processing location for bodies of fallen soldiers. A special building housed the coolers that held the remains, and the men who processed them often developed a soul-protecting, desensitized mindset as a result of their unfortunate MOS.

Marshall hung with those guys.

"You want to come see us do a body?" one of them offered.

"Man, I don't want to see that stuff. Get away from me." Marshall backed off.

He also saw and met infantrymen coming in from the field with scalps they had sliced off dead enemy soldiers' heads. These guys also taped the victims' hair to their helmets.

These fools are loco.

War can do that to a person—make them do things so out of the norm that they are never again the same. Marshall saw lots of those soldiers with black hair taped to their helmets. They also wore necklaces made from human ears. The body parts hung as warped badges of honor.

"Hey, Marshall, you want me to bring you a couple ears?"

The men had no compunction about retaliation. The scalps and ears signified to the enemy that if they messed with the Americans, the Americans would mess with them. Some took it too far, but only a combat soldier understood that mindset. Marshall accepted how it felt; a gang member assumed the same mindset. It protected them. It signified loyalty, and to them, it became a necessary part of their own personal war. These were the men with whom Marshall was assigned for his remaining time in-country. He delivered the orders that sent these men out on patrol. Whether or not they came back with scalps or ears remained beyond his purview and interest.

Marshall appreciated the chance to get back to the relative normalcy of An Khê for a short time before being sent back to Cam Ranh Bay. Almost time to rotate out. He completed eleven months and twenty-six days in Vietnam and saw a lot regarding the ways of the world. How can war not mature a man? He turned nineteen while in Nam, but in many ways, he had matured far beyond his years. He grew an old soul because of his experience, and he came home with a different perspective than when he left. Not only did Marshall have war in his heart, but he also carried disappointment because of the atrocities and bigotry he witnessed and experienced firsthand.

With a huge stash of weed, Marshall should have been ecstatic to return alive from Vietnam, but he hunched in his seat and refused to talk to anyone during the long flight to Hawaii. He developed some wonderful relationships with a few of his compatriots; they looked out for one another, cared for one another, and loved one another as wartime brothers. They lived and died for each other, and he missed them.

Who's going to look out for me now?

His thoughts centered on the journey and what would be waiting for him in the States. In many ways, the adventure enthralled him, and he fixed on his upcoming revolution.

Maybe I'll find me some bubbas to start a revolt.

PART TWO

FROM ONE MESS TO ANOTHER

CHAPTER SEVEN

HOMELAND RAGE

Marshall carried not only a Black man's anger but also a soldier's anger. As he stepped off the plane and into the airport during their refueling stop in Hawaii, he and his weary brothers' happiness at landing on American soil evaporated. Protestors greeted them. He kept his head down. He considered these protesters ignorant civilians; and, if he looked one in the eye, he might have lunged at him. As he entered the nearest bathroom, he saw scrawled across the wall an inflammatory bit of graffiti that stoked his rage to flamethrower level: *I hate n_____.*

He charged out of the bathroom, glared at the protesters, and strode back onto the plane. As he sat in his seat, he reflected on his life, and he knew his growth as an American and as a Black man encompassed more than his inner convictions. Society got uglier, and he longed to be a change agent, a militant one.

What does this look like for me, a Black man—a Black soldier in a country that values neither one? How can I help make changes in a country that involves others in a war for democracy and the fight for rights? All the while, they treat us like anything but equal citizens. Marshall spent the remainder of his journey home planning a militant uprising with his Black brothers and sisters. These ideals he really believed in his heart. He loved his country and so wanted not to be disappointed, but he grew disillusioned now that his eyes were opened to the way things really were.

I'm an American!

I fought for my country!

I wasn't drafted; I went of my own free will!

What happened to the world that valued people like Audie Murphy and John Wayne, and me?

Marshall saw the sacrifice of his boyhood heroes fade into resentment. He carried no shame as a soldier; he proudly wore his uniform and gained pride when he made it through basic. He had been pleased but afraid to be shipped to Vietnam, yet he knew he was a responsible part, a cog, that drove the military machine. He had been willing to die for his country. He now knew the depths of the change he envisioned for America and its values. Warfare bred hypocrisy, and Marshall was a conflicted man.

Marshall arrived at the small airport in Youngstown to nothing. No one waited, no family, no friends, not even protesters. He found a payphone and called his sister to come pick him up for his lukewarm homecoming. He said nothing about no one coming to greet him; he just wanted to, well, be.

During his thirty-day leave, he caught up with family and friends. The family made up for their airport absence by giving him a homecoming party with a special cake. He was surprised and delighted. While his relationship with his parents had grown peaceful, their spousal bond was the same; Ruthie had her boyfriend, and Ed had his alcohol. Ruthie spoon-fed her husband a little drink before work, so he could function, and she prepared a drink for him when he got home. All Marshall's siblings visited during the party except Abdul (James), who landed in a New York state prison.

Man, Marshall thought, *same old, same old. What did I expect, though?*

He, like many soldiers before him, had a hard time adjusting to life after Vietnam; everything was different. The jungle he now saw consisted of broken concrete and abandoned cars. In his imagination, he often smelled dung-fueled fires and saw snipers in the neighborhood. Everyone seemed glad to see him, but he felt they all wanted a piece of him. He partied his whole leave and continued to get high with the large stash he brought back from Nam. His brother Watdell got into it and left Marshall with much less than he brought, but he knew where to get more. With the weed came stateside connections and parties. The revelries included women, lots of women, and Marshall didn't ask about, nor go see, Joyce and his son.

Within their culture, things changed for Blacks in America. Proud of their heritage and looks, they grew out their hair naturally. Nappy, longer hair was in. Previously, White people made Marshall and other Blacks feel ashamed of themselves and how they looked, so they sometimes used processes to straighten their hair. They felt Whites looked down on Black hair in its natural state as ugly—something bad. Blacks of the sixties emerged from that sense of shame to announce, "Say it loud—I'm Black and I'm proud," and "Black is beautiful." Marshall enjoyed these new attitudes. Combing his hair out was not allowed in the Army, so he had to wait until his final year, which would be spent stateside, was up.

While home, Marshall watched news reports that chronicled the war and civil-rights protests. Now it was on TV in living color. He read much about the Black movement and spent a lot of time talking with other Black men about how they could affect change in America. This was a mission he wanted to be a part of, and even help lead if he could. He drew up plans in his mind about how to organize.

As his thirty-day leave ended, Marshall's reluctance to return to service grew. His disillusionment with all things smacking of White authority further fueled his growing rage, and to him, the Army was the height of White man's authority. A glowing fuse, Marshall stoked his fire with his new heroes: the Black nationalists, Malcolm X, and Stokely Carmichael. They advocated for Blacks to be separate from the ruling class and relate, instead, to Africa, their spiritual home. Marshall's mind exploded with the hate that racism wrought, and he wanted revenge for everything his people had endured in America.

Unlike the peaceful protests advocated by Martin Luther King Jr., the Black nationalists and the Black Panthers planned militant protests and, if possible, takeovers. Marshall supported them all, yet underneath he still had a sense of loyalty, which was now split between serving his country and serving his fellow Black countrymen. He signed up to serve in the Army, and so his remaining time would be used partly to help outfit his needs for a revolution.

Vietnam would not leave him; it added ugly pages to his history. Soldiers who returned from that arena of war had a saying: "When I die, I'm going to heaven because I done spent my time in hell." Marshall lived it, and he held it all in, but the pressure was growing. Yes, he prepared for a social, militant war, but he needed a release for the mixture of probable post-traumatic stress disorder (PTSD) and Black man's rage. He still had the remainder of the dynamite marijuana from Nam, the only thing that quelled his anger. Marshall called it dynamite because it was uncut, pure, and not mixed with fillers. To him, it kicked butt.

At the time of his report date back to duty in Fort Knox, Kentucky, Marshall's family headed to Alabama to visit family, so they took him along and dropped him off at the base.

Once back and settled, he went to the nearby town of Elizabethtown (E-Town) to buy a gun and a car, in that order. He bought plenty of ammo for his new weapon, a lightweight, compact .25 caliber pistol, and he carried it with him, concealed. It is one of the most dangerous handguns because when it fires a bullet into a person, the bullet "runs." It enters one spot and moves around inside the body.

The car was a novelty for a soldier; not many had one for personal use. With it, Marshall made frequent runs into town.

He considered himself prepared, on the offensive. He believed it likely that trouble would come for him, especially as a Black man in the South. He could have used the gun on anybody; he didn't care who. Hard-core and mean, Marshall still considered himself a killer, and his countenance caused people to keep their distance. By then, he had few friends, even Black ones. He'd lost track of Judd after basic, and Frank had long been reassigned elsewhere. Thus ended the roster of people Marshall felt he could wholeheartedly trust.

Marshall hung out with a few like-minded people during his time in Kentucky, but he kept even them at arm's length. He didn't let anyone get too close. Marshall let in someone occasionally, but only for protection. He figured a buffer would be good for him, someone who could either clear his way or be a lookout for him.

The new Black draftees came in with more knowledge of the world and more militancy.

Marshall learned more about the protests and their leaders from these men.

With all of that going on, it was hard for Marshall to get back into the regimented lifestyle of a soldier on an Army base in the States. Things like ordered drill and exacting uniform standards were lax in Vietnam, and Marshall balked at the return to the strict, organized roll call and duty regimen. Some things were ignored, including Marshall being AWOL (Absent Without Official Leave). Coming south with his family instead of through military channels on his way to base made him a week overdue to report for duty, but he faced no consequences. It was a pattern set by men returning from Asia. He didn't care.

CHAPTER EIGHT

REVOLUTION AND REALITY

While at Fort Knox, Marshall's assignment led to TDY (temporary duty) at armor school. In addition to being in an ordnance unit, Marshall obtained a new MOS and training on an M60 tank. The M60 weighed in at fifty tons of steel and mounted a 105-mm rifled gun and a fifty-caliber machine gun. In Marshall's mind, it was freakin' awesome! The powerful tank was capable of running straight through buildings and over houses—not a great weapon to place in the hands of an angry Black militant.

Marshall knew his ammo, and now he knew how to operate a fifty-plus-ton weapon mounted with a huge gun.

This is exactly what I need to do the White man some real harm.

He had wild thoughts about overthrowing the U.S. government (because the people in it were White and had control over him). His plan centered on how he could start the revolution that formed in his mind and get real power for Black folks. He knew power is never taken; it is always conceded. Marshall kept his distance from his commanding officers while at Fort Knox as he complied and did only enough to avoid drawing attention. But he knew *they* knew he embodied trouble looking for a place to happen.

After three months in Fort Knox, the Army offered Marshall the opportunity to take his next TDY either in the country of Panama or New York state. Most soldiers returning from Nam preferred not to return to a hot, coastal location. Marshall felt the same, so Panama was out for him. He only hesitated when he thought about the drugs he could score there. In March 1968, orders in his duffel, Marshall drove his car to Camp Drum just outside Watertown, New York. The small, resort-like community sat just over thirty miles south of Canada, with the Adirondacks and the gateway to the Thousand Islands tourist area nearby.

At Camp Drum, Marshall became part of a unit that trained "weekend warriors," the term regular soldiers derogatorily gave National Guard Reserve troops who came in on various weekends. Marshall, placed in ordnance, issued ammo to the "warriors" to use for their weekend games (exercises in military operations).

While in that opportune position, Marshall stole ammo for his take-over plans. His "take" included dynamite, grenades, and ammunition of all sorts. He hid his cache, told no one about it, and kept his plans in his head so no evidence could be traced to him.

I'm serious. I wonder how far I can take this.

Marshall wanted as much bang for his buck as he could get, so he continued to hide his contraband weapons. At that time, his efforts remained solo. He organized, kept to himself, and stayed on the lookout for like-minded Black men to join him once he got out of the service.

At that time, Marshall had a ganglion cyst on his hand, a swelling or tumor usually found on a joint near the wrist. When the men fell out in the morning, if a guy felt sick or had an issue, he could get a med callout. Marshall told his superiors about his cyst, and they sent him to a military hospital in Ayer, Massachusetts, to get it removed. The screams of amputees and men suffering from PTSD surrounded Marshall every day he was there.

Oh, man, what have I gotten myself into?

While in the hospital, Marshall floundered in the bureaucratic system—easy to do with the war still going on—so his surgical procedure hadn't taken place. He spent five weeks luxuriating in doing nothing. He rested, planned, and left the hospital every night to hang out downtown and look for women. He played it for all he could until the system caught up with him.

"Brandon, it's time we get your surgery scheduled," the doctor said.

"Nah, it's okay. I can live with it," Marshall said. That ended his "vacation" from his post.

Once the system found him, Marshall got shipped back to Camp Drum, pronto. When he got back, he and his commander, a temporary CO, continually disagreed. Marshall's growing anger manifested into a severe challenge to anyone in authority. His militancy unveiled, Marshall's conformity to orders was suspect at the least—unwilling at best.

Marshall faced repeated run-ins with a Black draftee out of Minnesota. His name was Mezcalf, and his actions bordered on bullish, too much so for Marshall, who never backed down from a fight, even with a fellow Black man.

Mezcalf started in on him. "Yo, pretty boy. What you doing hanging with them White girls in town?"

"Mezcalf," Marshall said, "who you calling pretty? You're just jealous. Right, boy?"

Marshall put extra emphasis on the word *boy*, wanting to see what Mezcalf had in him. He'd experienced the rancor before—draftees had disdain for soldiers who willingly registered to serve. He looked at Metcalf with his full dog on, which time in Vietnam had enhanced with frown lines too deep for time to erase.

"You got a car, so you probably have to buy your women," Metcalf grumbled as he backed away.

"Man, you don't know nothing. Nothing."

They didn't fight, but Marshall knew Mezcalf was just jealous. He chose to let it lie, physically. The loud retorts persisted.

When Mezcalf and Marshall later got into another shouting match, the sergeant sent Marshall to the temporary CO, a lieutenant. Walking into his office reminded Marshall of his trip to the CO's office in Bông So'n. He clenched his fists in memory of it and in anticipation of meeting with another White authority figure. The two of them stood alone in the lieutenant's office, and the officer made Marshall stand before him at attention as he sat and looked over the sergeant's report.

"I know you've been spending all your time downtown," said the CO.

In addition to going downtown at Ayer, Marshall drove to downtown Watertown often. "What's it to you?" Marshall said, "You can't keep me from going down there."

"If I catch you back down there, I'm going to break your neck."

"I better not see you downtown. I'll kill you."

The lieutenant took Marshall's threat seriously, having seen his anger rise with Mezcalf.

He called for more personnel to step into his office.

"This soldier just threatened me. He said he was going to kill me," the lieutenant told them.

Marshall countered, "I never said that to you. You just don't like me, do you? Come on, be honest; it's because I'm Black." Marshall knew he had him with his word against the officer's. Even though the CO outranked Marshall, the political and social climate dictated caution when a White man and a Black man had an altercation.

Marshall played the race card and won because right after he confronted him in front of witnesses, the lieutenant came over his desk at Marshall. The other officers had to constrain him. Marshall's smug look caused the CO to struggle against his restrainers, and they ushered Marshall out. No further action happened.

Marshall spent three months at Camp Drum, after which he returned to Fort Knox, his secret ammo/weapons dump still hidden in New York. With three months left in service, he counted the hours. He considered any time spent away from base a bonus, so Marshall drove a leisurely route back to Fort Knox. After he signed out from Camp Drum, he had a prescribed period to report. He arranged for another guy to sign him out and left early. He showed up at Knox within the timeframe of his falsified sign-out date, and on reporting for duty, a meeting with the new CO awaited him.

When Marshall walked into his office, there sat the lieutenant from Camp Drum, fresh from a promotion and reassignment.

Oh no, Marshall thought.

"Well, hello there, Private Brandon. How nice to see you again," the CO said with an icy smile that froze Marshall's tongue. "Thought you could get away with a false sign-out report, huh?"

Marshall knew he was had. He stood at attention and said nothing.

"Tell you what, private," said the CO, "I'm going to charge you with an Article Fifteen.

Man, this crap blows, Marshall thought.

That time Marshall received another minimal fine and received two weeks of extra duty. He was busted but not too upset because his time was short.

Marshall worked regular duty Monday through Friday from eight to four with most weekends off. He had relatives in nearby Louisville, and he wanted to hang with friendly Black folks. So he took the time to get to know his maternal Uncle Henry and his family on his weekends. A lot happened in Louisville, especially on the "drag" called Broadway, where lots of bars held Marshall's interest. Marshall hung out there a few times until his cousin Winston found out and told him he was chillin' in dangerous surroundings.

Winston lived in a nice house in the Louisville suburbs where Marshall often stayed on the weekends he went to town. He gave Marshall a key, so he could go and come as he pleased.

Marshall's Uncle Henry and Aunt Lil lived right across the Ohio River from Louisville in Jeffersonville, Indiana. Unlike the duplex in which Marshall grew up, their house seemed a mansion to him. A two-story structure with two bedrooms, it featured a medium-sized kitchen, dining room, and living room on the main floor. They also enjoyed a finished basement with a laundry room.

Uncle Henry does okay for an uneducated Black man from Alabama. Maybe I should investigate construction too.

Henry forged a reputation as a well-known community activist, and Aunt Lil was a strong Christian woman who sang and played the piano. Their house was filled with tuneful sounds because the children inherited the musical gene from Lil. Other relatives joined them on Sundays, and Marshall basked in the family love.

Aunt Lil boasted great cooking skills and always made plenty for guests. Every time Marshall arrived, he closed his eyes as he entered and breathed in the aromas of her good cooking. He got his fill of fried chicken, pork chops and gravy, biscuits, and green beans. He felt peaceful while there, and Aunt Lil kept Marshall's belly full of good stuff. He enjoyed a comfortable bed in their welcoming home.

Owning a car gave Marshall greater freedom, not only to visit his relatives but also during his evenings to swing into E-Town to see the ladies or go to a club. The lure and comfort of marijuana continued to encompass Marshall. During his final few months in the Army, he added a codeine-infused liquid cough syrup, which he bought from a pharmacy in town, into his daily routine. The combination served to slowly dull Marshall's senses, and his anger as well. His priorities shifted, although he didn't consciously realize it.

Marshall's antagonism toward Whites had deep roots, but not toward individuals. His hostility focused on the "White Machine" of rule and power that emanated from the government. He befriended White men on occasion. Because he missed having a close, trustworthy companion, he buddied up to a White man named Jerry, who served alongside him in Kentucky during his final months in the Army.

A skinny man, Jerry looked like he couldn't fight, much less be a soldier. He and Marshall visited bars in E-Town, and Jerry would instigate a fight between Marshall and another man. Jerry stepped in and hustled the man outside, and beat the crap out of him. Marshall either watched or joined in, depending on how Jerry handled the guy. It gave Marshall one of the many releases that helped mollify his rage.

Despite the hours he spent in the clubs, the time Marshall spent with Uncle Henry and Aunt Lillian became a good foundation for what a solid family life looked like. Since they were stable working people, it didn't occur to Marshall their behavior might be because they were Christians. They extended a love and warmth to him that his parents never did. Henry and Lillian had four children they brought up in the faith, but Henry explained to Marshall that Winston, their oldest, had since backslidden into a life of debauchery.

"Uncle Henry," said Marshall, "I don't understand what you mean."

"Marshall, you come out and sit on the swing with me." Henry reserved his most serious conversations for the porch. Flies buzzed in the background and sat on the rims of their iced tea glasses. Henry folded his gnarled mahogany hands in his lap.

"Young man, I've worked hard all my life. Your Aunt Lillian and me, we were both raised in the church. I love Jesus, and I love my wife." Henry took a long moment and stared at the old hunting dogs lounging in the shade of the historic oak tree that filled his front lawn. "When the good Lord gave us children, we dedicated them to Him. All of them made decisions to give their hearts to Jesus when they were little. Winston believed in Jesus, and his life, at least for a while, showed that he loved the Lord."

Marshall settled into his side of the swing. He knew this would take a while as he remembered what his mom said about Uncle Henry: "When he tells a story, best get comfortable because it's going to go on until he decides he's finished."

"Son, I don't know what happened," Henry began, "because all our other babies have given their hearts to Jesus; and they live by His Word. My Winston, he fell in with some people who led him astray. And now he doesn't go to church anymore. He made his choice, and now instead of serving the Lord, he serves liquor in those bars he owns."

Henry had been staring at the floor of the porch as he told Winston's story. Suddenly, he turned his focus to his nephew.

"Marshall, what are you going to do with this life the Lord gave you?"

"Sir?" Marshall had slipped into introspection. He thought Winston's life didn't seem so bad. *What's the problem with having a good time and a few bars? My life has not been a great ball of fun so far. Maybe Winston can connect me with more people.*

He decided right then to hang out with his cousin more often. That lifestyle appealed to Marshall because Winston had ready access to booze and women. His source for weed hailed from Louisville too. To Marshall, it looked like a win-win situation.

Marshall's reverie ended when his uncle tapped his shoulder. "Boy, you look like you got some kind of daydream going."

"Sir, thank you, but I think I might hang with Winston a while. He can help me make some money, and I know how to take care of myself."

With no trace of malice, Uncle Henry sighed and said, "See that you do, child."

He's calling me a child? Hmmph.

"Uncle Henry, you're a good man, and I appreciate all you and Aunt Lil have done for me. It's good you have your faith. But for me, I've got to make my way and prove myself. I've seen enough in the Army to know that it's a White man's world. I'd like to see what I can learn from Winston."

———————

Marshall liked that his cousin owned businesses, and he began part-time work as a doorman for him during his weekends off, collecting the cover charge from the bars' patrons. It inspired him to see a Black man succeed. While Marshall hung out with him, Winston encouraged him to take the postal service exam. Marshall enrolled in the Army-administered schooling to get his GED so that he could take the postal exam, which he passed.

Hey! I got another certificate. I finished something else!

He didn't know what he would do with it, but he thanked Winston as he spurred him to act on both.

The military powers-that-be tried to keep Marshall busy and out of trouble until his release date. While in school, they left him alone because he was otherwise occupied. In general, when a soldier reaches the two-month mark until discharge, the Army speaks to him about reenlisting. To Marshall, his reputation kept the Army from sending someone to talk to him about staying in. The Army seemed as eager to have him go as he was to wave bye-bye to the service.

On November 1, 1968, three years after boarding the plane to Fort Jackson, Marshall completed his military service and gained an honorable discharge from the Army.

"Free at last," he said as he drove away from the base.

CHAPTER NINE

FREE?

Winston wanted Marshall to stay and work the bars after he got out, or at least start work with the postal service. When Marshall had been only a few weeks away from getting out, Winston spoke to his cousin after a night at one of the bars and tried to persuade him to stay on after the Army.

"Marshall, why don't you stay and work with me?"

"Nah, man," Marshall said, "I gotta go back to Youngstown and visit my mom and family."

"You don't want to go back. You told me what it's like."

"Yeah, but I need to see my family first. It's my roots. I'll come back after I visit them."

"Nah, you won't, man."

Marshall's desire to go home was mostly to show both his parents that he had become something. He served his country and received an honorable discharge. He had his GED and had passed the postal service exam.

I am somebody. Now I just have to fit in someplace.

He intended to check in at home and then go back to Louisville because he really liked the stable environment and good money he earned while working with Winston. Another plus? The warmer weather. Moderate winters there beat Youngstown's harsh ones.

Intentions failed to keep Marshall from sinking into the quagmire of Youngstown, Ohio. It not only sucked him in; it sucked him under. He made plans to go to Cleveland to complete his postal service application, but he didn't even do that.

Once settled, he got a job in a steel mill—Youngstown Sheet and Tube— just like his father, who still labored there. As he worked, Marshall kept doing his thing. He got high, got a girlfriend, and now out of the Army, he got busy organizing Black folks for war. Being home brought back all the memories of suppression and abuse that he now blamed on racism.

Despite the numbing effects of the drugs, Marshall's demeanor spiked; he exuded a wildness that was off-putting even to the extremists he sought to enlist. He spoke like a revolutionary, and his manner and words scared people so much they backed away from him and his plans.

The marijuana bus rolled on, and when his old gang buddy Danny Bronn acquainted Marshall with morphine, it began the end of Marshall's run to revolution. Marshall didn't know squat about addiction; he only knew getting high made him feel good and calmed him. The more drugs he took, the less the anger that previously mastered him became a factor in his life. Drugs dominated him; they masked all his reawakened pain, anger, disillusionment, and common sense. He soon began to shoot morphine intravenously—then came heroin, the master lord over all his others.

It started when a friend gave him a free hit, which led to a long enough string of freebies to get him addicted. No more free rides. Now he had to buy it. He woke up every day with the question: *How do I get the money to buy my drugs today?*

He didn't make enough legitimate money to keep up his habit, and only a few weeks into his job at the steel mill, he walked into the break room and heard his paper lunch bag crackling. He looked in it and saw a huge rat trying to get at his cellophane-wrapped sandwich. "Not today, buddy," said Marshall, "I'm eating that lunch." He knocked the vermin in the head and watched it run off, leaving a bloody trail. After that, Marshall stayed only long enough at the steel mill job to find something else. He had to be employed, so he could support his habit.

He heard the Army was hiring civilians at a nearby munitions plant. With his background in ammo and chemical warfare, Marshall got a job working the line at the Ravenna Arsenal, an ammunition-production facility that operated during the Vietnam War. Marshall made forty-millimeter shells and eight-inch projectiles for the tanks and bombs used in the war. He continued to work even as his addiction grew, with one foot in the world of an addict and the other foot in the working world, trying to make money. He stayed rent-free at his parents' house, so he had enough to feed his drug habit.

On the line at his job, Marshall spied an attractive White woman. He looked at her and received the desired response: She flirted with him every time he caught her looking at him. It didn't bother him to date White women; they didn't represent authority. Marshall hadn't seen and barely thought about Joyce and his son, Keith. He fancied himself a free man with no responsibilities. Marshall discovered the White woman's name, Kendra, but they hadn't gotten past gazing at one another with interest and underlying intent. They only made eyes at each other and had brief, meaningless conversations because he remained cautious about a relationship with a White woman. He simply wanted to be close to her and hear her voice until he discerned, she wanted him sexually too.

One night she followed him home. He carpooled to save even more drug money, and when he got out of the car, he saw another car pull up to the curb behind them. Kendra was behind the wheel, and she invited him into her car, where they talked awhile.

The two began a wild affair, and Marshall fell in love with Kendra. He introduced her to his mother, and Ruthie was hospitable. Her one question to Marshall was whether her family welcomed him as Ruthie had Kendra. They did. They lived separately but often frequented motels during their torrid romance. At times Kendra slept at Ruthie's house on the living room sofa. The entire time Marshall continued strung out on drugs, and despite his deep feelings for Kendra, he played her. Staying high remained his priority, and he dwelt in a bad, ugly place. During one of their nightly soirees, Kendra announced, "Marshall, I'm pregnant."

He stared at her as if she said he had a piece of food stuck in his teeth. A truth, but one he felt was easily fixed. *Must get out of this situation.* "I'd like you to get an abortion."

"I'm going to have this baby, Marshall. With or without you."

"It's going to be without me, baby."

Kendra accepted his rebuttal with, "I'll put it up for adoption. I can't raise a child by myself."

"Fine by me."

Marshall backed off from her just as he had backed off from Joyce. His love had conditions after all. Marshall told Ruthie, and she asked her son to own up to his responsibilities.

She continued to show a surprising interest in Kendra's welfare, as she had for Joyce and her child.

When Marshall didn't step up, even after returning home, Ruthie, in a show of the nurturing Marshall rarely saw as a child, often babysat Keith. Marshall avoided the house when he knew his mom had babysitting duty. He dumped his responsibility on his mother, assuming she would take it. His interest lay elsewhere.

In 1969, Marshall did everything he could to stay high, Kendra and the baby forgotten.

"Marshall, I know what you're doing," said his mother. "Don't think you can hide it from me. Please stop doing the drugs."

"Mom, I'm fine. Just leave me alone."

"You can't stay here anymore if you are on drugs. But if you get yourself into a treatment center, I will let you stay."

With nowhere else to go, Marshall agreed. At that time, drug addicts had few places to get help, and he went only because his mother wouldn't leave him alone. He checked himself into Woodside Hospital's drug program in Youngstown. He wanted out right away, but even though a patient could write himself in and out of the facility, they wouldn't let him out of lockdown. He thought he'd ended up in a real nut house because the effects of withdrawal made things worse. He tolerated methadone, a drug used to wean addicts off heroin, and endured individual and group therapy sessions. He only wanted one thing—out.

He finally called his mother. "Mom, they won't let me out of here."

"Are you well, Son?"

"I'm fine, Mom. Just come get me out of here."

And she did. Two hellish weeks after going in, he walked out.

"I'm never doing that again," Marshall told his mother. He didn't like going anywhere he couldn't leave.

He said all the right things to his mom and anyone else who questioned his state of mind, but he continued his trek into the drug abyss. He made no attempt at all to continue what rehab started. As an addict, he existed on a high. Without the drugs, he fell into sickness. That cycle kept him on the drugs; he couldn't turn back then, even if he wanted to. The drugs were his medicine he needed to stay functional.

His stint in Woodside ended his job at the arsenal, so Marshall had to figure out how to get more cash. He shoplifted and did everything else he could think of to make enough money to stay stoned.

Heroin is an insidious foe; if it's cut with too much other stuff, the high lasts a shorter time. The purer it is, the longer the euphoria. What Marshall took varied from short bouts to a high of up to six or seven hours. He took hits throughout each day until his money disappeared. His immediate battle caused him to work and make enough money to get high and spend every cent on heroin. No extra money was kept for food or gas; he borrowed all he could from friends and family until he tapped them out.

Marshall reconnected with some of his old gang members that summer, and his brother Abdul joined the mix. The group, however, developed far from the revolutionary one he had his heart set on when he returned from Nam. Instead of Black power, drug power ruled him. Marshall and his drug gang had little money. Most worked relatively low-paying jobs, so they started talking about how to rake in enough cash to keep supplied with the drugs they needed.

Nothing was out of bounds—nothing.

The gang hung out in a place called the shooting gallery where they met to do drugs, party, have sexual liaisons, and plan their next heist. The house was one step above ramshackle and haunted a lot down the street from Marshall's parents. A lady named Miss Hattie bought the house for herself and her kids. She hustled White Lightning (illegal, homemade whiskey), hosted gambling games, and sold some drugs. She did what she had to do to survive, albeit illegally. Miss Hattie emceed crap games and paid guys to help her run them. Pimps frequented the place, and her husband and boyfriend both lived in the house at various, yet separate, times.

Marshall and the guys knew shoplifting wouldn't sustain their drug use, so they planned bigger scores to bring in more money. Abdul scoped lucrative places to rob, and he came in one night and said he'd found an easy mark. Marshall trusted his older brother's experience and street smarts, so he agreed with whatever Abdul was planning. Abdul cased a jewelry store and thought it perfect for them. Marshall and his friends, Woogie and Cadillac, were all in.

With Abdul leading and Marshall driving, the four of them went to the jewelry store one day at dusk. They entered, unmasked, through the front door.

"Hey, you got some nice things," Abdul said to the clerk.

"Yeah, you all want to see something?"

They pulled their guns and Abdul said, "This is a stick-up."

"Get in back of the store." Marshall pointed with his gun as he edged the salesclerk toward the rear of the building. Abdul, Woogie, and Cadillac pulled merchandise out of the cases as Marshall kept the guy in back.

"Get down on the floor," Marshall ordered the shopkeeper. "Don't say a thing until we're gone."

A mere five minutes passed, and they ran out the front door, oblivious to anything but getting to their car. Marshall jumped into the driver's seat, panting; he fumbled with the keys. "Man! Move it, Marshall!" the guys screamed at him. Marshall floored the gas pedal, but as soon as he got out of the block, he slowed to legal speed. His sweaty hands slid on the steering wheel, and he wiped them on his pants and slammed the brakes as he took the next corner. A police squad with blaring lights and siren screamed past them; Marshall froze as he watched it pass.

"Marshall! Marshall!" yelled his brother. "Keep going."

Eyes on the rearview mirror and knees quavering, Marshall clenched the steering wheel and eased out of the block toward safety.

Fear replaced Marshall's bravado. Woodside gave him a glimpse of being locked away and he thought, *What if I end up in jail?*

The shooting gallery operated as their safe house—an environment to debrief and assess their haul. They shut and locked the door of an unused room and put their haul on a table.

Abdul looked it over and said, "Whoa, we hit the mother lode." "What do we do now?" asked Woogie.

"I know a fence," said Abdul. "He can take it and sell it for us."

Caution forgotten in the sight of such riches, they headed to the fence to get cash. His place sat a few blocks from the jewelry store. They figured by the time they got there, the police would be gone, and they could get in and out with no attention drawn.

Each guy changed his clothes, and they left after dark in a different car. Unknown to them, someone witnessed the four drive off from the robbery and described what they saw to the police—a car carrying four Black men. As soon as Marshall and the guys entered the neighborhood, the police, who were still in the area, lit them up with searchlights.

Marshall slid the car into a walled drive, and Cadillac threw the bag holding the jewelry over a fence. Their guns followed, and Cadillac ran. The police pulled in right after they tossed the evidence. The officers pointed their guns at Marshall, Woogie, and Abdul.

One officer stood calm and confident and held his gun at Marshall's eye level.

He asked, "Where you guys been?"

Marshall started to run, but Abdul held him by his jacket. "Don't run. It's okay; I've got this."

Abdul then gave the cops some story Marshall didn't follow. Marshall, this being his first robbery, trusted Abdul to get them out of it since he had already been in jail and supposedly knew the ropes.

The next thing Marshall knew, six to eight cop cars surrounded them, and the police cuffed them. Since they'd thrown the bag and guns, the police possessed no direct evidence. The other three guys didn't know it, but Cadillac watched from a darkened alley across the street. After the police hauled Marshall, his brother, and Woogie off and towed their car, he ran back over and grabbed the bag of jewelry and guns.

"Man, Abdul," said Marshall in the back of the squad car, "I thought you knew what you were doing."

Abdul grunted.

At the Youngstown City Jail, the witness came forward and identified the three as the ones who committed the armed robbery. Marshall thought it a setup because the store sat at least twenty feet back from the road and an old White lady witnessed it. Marshall wondered how she could have seen enough in the dark to describe three Black men. The police accepted her testimony and locked up all three men.

Yeah, even old White women have it out for us Black men, Marshall mused as a policeman shoved him into a cell.

In 1970 the city jail was a grim environment. Wads of spit and blood stained the cement floors, and Marshall didn't want to sit on the grungy seat but had no other choice. *Man, this is worse than Nam. People. Use soap. Man!*

Except for his overnight in the Army stockade in Nam, Marshall had little experience with jail. Yet there he sat, busted for armed robbery. No mattresses graced the steel bunks, and several drunks in the holding cell decorated it with vomit and pee, some on the floor and walls, but most of it on them. As Marshall sat in the lockup, he looked with disgust at the horrid place and tried to figure out how to get out of this situation. He and Abdul cooled their heels in the same cage, and Marshall used his phone call to contact their mom.

Ruthie blamed Abdul for getting Marshall started on drugs and robbery. She later told him he should have been a better example for young Marshall.

Ruthie and Kendra combined their money to get Marshall out on bond, but it took the police until the next day to release him. Abdul and Woogie remained in jail. Marshall's relationship with his mother—no longer a scab—wore itself into a smooth scar. Through everything, he loved her, and when he gained her respect by standing up to her, their relationship revealed the love. Even though the family remained dysfunctional, he and his mother were close. Marshall knew Kendra's help enabled his mom to spring him. Not enough money remained to get Abdul released.

Those overnight hours in the city jail partially detoxed Marshall, but not enough to cleanse him. He knew in his heart he would be sent to prison, so he took all the drugs he could before he went. He knew he broke his mother's heart, but he couldn't stop. While out on bond, Kendra gave birth to their child. She called him from the hospital. "Marshall, we have a baby girl."

"What?" With a momentary lapse of his resolve to step away, he said, "Oh, man. I'll come by and see her."

"She looks like you."

Marshall lied. He didn't go near the hospital—had no intention of going. He wanted to leave any semblance of responsibility in his past.

The jury found Marshall guilty, and his mother was too emotional to go to the sentencing, so Eva went to support him. As he stood before the judge, Marshall said, "Sir, I am a soldier; I just got back from Vietnam."

"Okay, son, welcome home. You are now going to prison."

CHAPTER TEN

NO WAY OUT

Because of Marshall's young age of twenty-one, the sentence imposed was ten to twenty-five years at the Ohio State Reformatory in Mansfield, while Abdul received a sentence twice as long at the Ohio State Penitentiary in Columbus.

With only three days to get his business in order, Marshall loaded up on drugs as if the residue would carry him through the duration. Only the fear of punishment on arrival kept him from indulging on his last free day before he reported to the bailiff at the courthouse.

The scene at his mother's house on April 1, 1970, portrayed razor-sharp emotion. Ruthie cried. Eva cried. Marshall cried. His dad was absent.

That day, Marshall boarded a van bound for the reformatory, 130 miles from home and countless miles from where he thought he'd be as a soldier returning from serving his country. With a gut-wrenching expletive exploding in his throat, Marshall thought, *I never started my revolution.*

He looked out the window at his sister as the van drove off, hoping for a last-minute reprieve, but none came. He fell beyond the scope of his family's help. It proved hard enough dealing with the knowledge of such a long sentence; he also had officially started withdrawal from the drugs. His body revolted after only two days' absence. Nauseated and in pain, Marshall felt his anxiety level rise beyond the red line. He had nothing to help ease all he was feeling.

Marshall, in jeans and an old T-shirt, was shackled to his buddy Cadillac, the one who ran the night of the robbery. Cadillac was busted later for a different infraction. Their arms were interlocked at the elbows, and each wore handcuffs. The cuffs were attached to a chain around their waists, and iron shackles grated skin off their ankles and allowed only shuffle steps. All four of the prisoners on the van were so bound, and the two guards kept alert for anything awry. Marshall was as white-knuckle scared as a Black man could get.

How am I going to get out of this?

The Ohio State Reformatory (OSR) opened for its first 150 prisoners in 1896. By the time Marshall entered, thousands of prisoners had lived within its walls, some never to leave. Imposing in its Gothic appearance and constructed of limestone and iron, the OSR had the largest freestanding cell block in the world, six tiers high. Originally built as a boys' reformatory, it housed its own power station and a working farm.

Marshall shuddered when he saw the imposing edifice, and he bent over as much as he could without pulling over his shackle-mate. *I can't stay here ten years. God, help me!*

This prison—despite looking like a castle—was full of everything but fairy tales. Demons of despondency greeted Marshall as he exited the vehicle with the other inmates. He shuffled into his new home in the fetters that affixed him to Cadillac, and the guard who greeted them immediately stripped him of his cuffs, chains, foot shackles, clothes, and any remaining pride.

"You're going to love what's next, maggots," said the guard.

Am I back in the Army? Marshall wondered as he gave the man a double take in case he was having a walking nightmare.

Bug spray.

What the—?

The razor-like jet of decontaminant cut into his skin and made him jerk as he tried to keep his face and eyes away from the poison. After his humiliating disinfection, the guards shaved his newly grown afro and goatee, then made him don a set of white coveralls—which identified him as a new inmate—and a pair of prison-issued boots, brown brogans.

The guards took them on the long walk down the corridor toward the orientation area. Marshall looked at Cadillac and the two inmates who walked ahead of them. He couldn't see past the guard who strutted in front of them, but as he twisted his neck, he caught sight of the one who followed at their heels. He leaned into Cadillac to avoid rubbing shoulders with the guard to his right. Cadillac squeezed in, trying to do the same with the guard to his left.

Each set of steel doors took him further into the depths of a morass of fear and confusion. The lead guard's keys jangled as he walked, and Marshall's footsteps matched those of Cadillac as they echoed down the passageway. Sweat ran down his spine and from his armpits. He didn't look up—just kept his eyes on the legs moving in front of him. The concrete gave evidence of the many men who had shuffled past, with deep marks worn by countless shoes and dragged chains.

The guard opened one set of large steel doors, and the group edged through. *Wham!* Marshall heard the rear guard slam and lock the door behind them. Same thing at the second set of doors. As it shut, the sound reverberated into Marshall's soul. *Wham!* When they went through the third set of steel doors that opened into the center of the institution, the guard slammed the door shut behind them and locked it with a sound Marshall swore he'd never forget.

Whoo-wham!

Welcome to a darker place.

The bullpen encompassed a large open area—the crux of the cellblocks—on the ground floor. Going anywhere within the prison meant crossing through there. All new prisoner orientation took place on the first tier. The guard they called Lieutenant Red stood on a stand in the center and directed the march of the new inmates, just as he directed all goings-on within the bullpen. Marshall looked up at the vast, thirty-foot walls and cringed as he bore the verbal assault of the inmates already housed in the cells. To Marshall, it looked like all of them had their dogs on.

A prisoner he came to know as Scat called out, "Hey, new boy, we're gonna get to you. Don't try to hide. We'll find you."

The guards, charged with keeping the newbies safe, yelled at the prisoners in the cells, "Shut up! Get to the back of your cells and shut up!" The language both groups used matched their ferocity. Marshall caught the sound of words even he hadn't heard before.

Ugly memories of childhood flooded back to Marshall as the guards led him to his cellblock. He winced at the recollection of his mother telling him to shut up as she locked him in the closet. As he thought of that, he also tried to wrap his mind around getting out.

How do I get out of here? How am I supposed to protect myself until I do?

"Hey, boy, you look pretty good. I'm sure we'll get it on before you leave here." All the guys hooted and hollered at each new crop of inmates. "Hey, boys. You got a man?" Despite his toughness, fear filled Marshall. He knew each of those guys considered himself the baddest man on the planet. Marshall's main concern now rested in self-protection, and he knew he had to buckle down and plan a strategy for survival.

Again, he wondered silently, *How am I going to make it? How am I going to survive this?*

Am I going to have to kill somebody in here?

He surprised himself at his readiness to do so if he had to.

First-day orientation meant getting fingerprinted and classified as inmate number 78961. Straining his neck to see the number on his prison garb, he felt white-hot tears well up, tears he sniffled back so others wouldn't see.

This number, I'm not proud to wear.

What a difference from the great pride he felt when looking at his name on his Army uniform. His pride turned to shame, but no way would he display weakness, for to do so would open him up to abuse. He straightened up and continued with the process, hardening himself even through the drug withdrawal he endured.

He shuffled to a two-person cell in the six-tier structure's southeast corner, segregated according to the social norms of the time. The cell-block—the foreboding section—spoke to Marshall as he scraped in: *Your life will never be the same.*

Marshall's small area consisted of a steel bunk bed with a thin mattress and threadbare sheets. The favored top bunk was already inhabited by a guy who chose not to acknowledge Marshall on the first night.

Is that gray blob a pillow? Ugh.

Grey from repeated attempts at cleaning, the flimsy cushion also bore ghostly shadows from blood, sweat, and, yes, tears. A chipped porcelain commode with no lid and oily-looking water balanced in the corner, threatening to tip. Alongside it sat a simple, white sink with rusted faucets. A small desk sat along a dank, graffiti-covered wall.

Who's going to want to hear from me?

As he lay on his cot that first night, he thought about his sentence, and he despaired he would have to stay in longer than ten years.

How can I do twenty-five years? What does my life mean now?

He went to sleep surrounded by the sounds of muffled crying and catcalls. He covered his face with the thin pillow and tried to keep his movements silent on the creaky bed as he settled in, seeking to be invisible in sight and sound.

A thirty-day orientation introduced the men to life in the OSR. Marshall learned all about jail—what he needed to do and the rules for what not to do. All new inmates had to read the handbook, and while he broke many rules at home and in the Army, he now knew every infraction could cost him another year in that hell. To him, it served as a trauma ward, and he detoxed while he learned what to do to survive in the madness of a new environment. The guards isolated the newbies for protection from the seasoned inmates. Along the way, he ran into others from the old hood, which brought some calm to his distress.

During an inmate's first week, a skills assessment leads to job assignments. Inmates could work or choose to lie idle. If a guy chose the latter, he only left his cell to eat. Marshall decided to work; laziness wouldn't work for him. One of the hallmarks at the OSR was vocational training for the men, and in that, the inmates did everything but run the place. Marshall received duty in the identification (ID) department. When new guys came in, he gathered their information and typed out their ID-numbered badges. Once his thirty-day orientation ended, and he had a regular job, Marshall happily gave up his white coveralls and put on prison blues—blue pants and blue shirt.

His typical day began with roll call at 7:00 a.m. Each tier of cells had rolling doors along one track controlled with a crank by the guards. When the doors slid open, the inmates had to stand outside their cells as the guard on duty tallied the men to make sure no one had escaped since the last count, which took place at the end of each guard's shift. The doors shut quickly, and no one wanted to be partway out when the doors slammed. Getting caught could result in a crushed hand. OSR served a fast breakfast right after roll call; the men had a full fifteen minutes to grab their trays of food, eat, and dump the remainder. By 7:30 or 7:45, Marshall reported for his job at the ID station, just off the bullpen.

His job hours included a lunch break with a roll call at his cell and an hour in the yard, the outdoor area where prisoners could get fresh air, recreation, conversation, and relaxation time. His workday ended at 3:00. Supper was in the evening, and the third and last roll call of the day took place at 8:00 each night.

Marshall, a seasoned and resourceful man, quickly learned the ropes. He kept his eyes open, and he listened and stayed out of trouble. Yard time included many conversations with other guys, and he learned the first two rules of being in prison: don't gamble, and don't become beholden to anyone. If a guy offered a pack of cigarettes, the payback usually included interest—two packs of cigarettes.

After his initial fear, Marshall toughened his stance and backed down from no one who wanted to test his mettle. As a result, he gained a lot of respect from the other inmates. He was the de facto leader of those who came in from Youngstown because they knew his reputation from the hood. Having a group around him helped cement his position as a leader within the walls of Mansfield. Marshall knew he would be tested every day and that any show of weakness could lead to exploitation by the other men. He put his dog on 24/7.

After Marshall's first three days of detoxing, he was weak but feeling better. His cellmate, a bodybuilder, was new to the OSR but not to prison life. He taught Marshall how to work out and get back into shape. He used the on-site gym, and as the drugs in his system wore off, his physique grew stronger.

I will not get back on drugs when I get out of here. I will not *come back here.*

He hoped he could stay straight and get out sooner than his sentence dictated.

His "Black Binge," as he called it, resurfaced once the drugs exited his system. He again sought to expand the scope of Black men's power within America. This time, however, it came through diplomacy and social change, not militancy. One of the guys spoke with Marshall about taking an African name. He gave Marshall the Swahili name Kali, meaning "fierce" and "sharp," a title Marshall bore with great pride. He learned and lived out a bit of Swahili, too: *nguvu zone kea mtg mweusi*, which means "all power to the Black man."

Marshall and some others started an approved club—the Black Culture Club—and had their own room for meetings. They decorated it as best they could with magazine pages and later changed the name to the African

American Culture Club. Through use of their commissary money earned from prison jobs, they brought in materials that spoke to their interests, books by Eldridge Cleaver and Malcolm X and literature sent by Black nationalists and the Black Panthers. Once again, propaganda added to Marshall's knowledge of what happened in the world outside—this time from prison.

Marshall knew how to influence people, and because of his leadership within the prison, he became president of the African American Culture Club. In title, it was a club yet, in essence, a gang. He presided over a hundred guys who did whatever he asked of them. Only a man with a death wish would mess with the club or Marshall. Each club had an outside advisor, and Marshall's group was saddled with an anxious man who did not trust them. He told them he knew they were going to run (try to escape from incarceration). None of them ever did.

The prison bully tried to goad Marshall into a fight to gain control over him, but Marshall wouldn't submit. The man would yell at Marshall from the cellblock across the way.

"Come over and fight, Marshall. You got nothing on me," the bully would shout, with his flunkies flanking him.

"Nah, man, if you want to fight, you come over here, just you and me."

Marshall knew the bully's tactic was to get him alone and have his lackeys beat him. Marshall didn't back down because he knew that one on one he could beat the guy. The bully would soon find out.

CHAPTER ELEVEN

A WAY OUT?

Larry was one of the other prisoners who joined the African American Culture Club, and Marshall learned he possessed some college training. He ran into Larry in the club's library, listening to some records.

"Hey, Larry. What's that?"

"Man, this guy's the best. It's John Coltrane. That cat blows a mean sax. Here, listen." Marshall settled in as Larry turned up the volume. He watched Larry's reaction to the music.

"How'd you hear about him?"

"Started listening to him in college, man."

Marshall thought about how cool it would have been to go to college.

"You were in college? How'd you end up here?"

Larry listened to the music for a minute before he replied, "Got caught up in drugs, and it messed me up. I got busted for armed robbery."

"Me, too, man. No more of that for me." Marshall closed his eyes as he listened to 'Trane.

"What'd you learn in college?" Marshall wanted more stuff to dream on. Larry rubbed his hands over his chin and said, "I write poetry and plays."

"What?" marveled Marshall.

"Yeah," Larry mused, "It's why I went to school. I love writing— and directing."

"You don't act?"

"Nah, I like to stay behind the scenes."

Marshall never thought of himself as a thespian, but something inside made him ask.

"Think I could be in one of your plays? I mean, our club could sponsor one."

Larry clasped his hands together as if praying and said, "Now that's what I'm talking about.

Let's do this."

The themes of all of Larry's works had to do with Black peoples' freedom from oppression—from White authority and the tribulations it wrought. Not a few men tried out for roles, and when he auditioned, Marshall usually garnered a lead role. As he acted, he relished how free it made him feel. For a while, he relinquished his militant posture and poured himself into the roles.

Hey, I like this theater stuff, Marshall thought as he rehearsed in the prison gym. He did well in the plays, and Larry, as well as other actors and members of the audience, complimented him on his ability. He vowed to focus on that when he got out.

Marshall remained social yet careful while in prison. His newfound intellectual competence helped him realize there was more to life than fighting and gangs.

Marshall's abysmal home life squashed his initial love of learning discovered in elementary school. Exposure to something outside of domestic strife reinstated his interest in a better life.

In the yard one day, he asked an old-timer how to succeed on the inside.

"What's it like in here? What do I have to do to get ahead? I'm not into doing nothing and letting the system drag me down. I want to improve myself and get ready for when I get out. I gotta keep strong."

"You know, man. Get yourself a job that will train you to get work on the outside." Marshall questioned other men about what they did for work within the OSR. The inmates kept it running by working jobs in laundry, landscaping, maintenance, the commissary, as hospital assistants, and other facilities-related work. Marshall checked out the Power House because others told him no one who worked in that area ever lost out on parole. The Power House generated all the energy required for the electrical demands of the facility.

Marshall kept an eye out for vacancies within that department, and when one appeared, he applied. His Army background helped with his skills assessment, and after six months at the ID department, he earned a job "making electricity." For over a year, Marshall worked at the Power House and used his training well. He took a State of Ohio test and received certification as a stationary engineer—a role that encompassed all aspects of boiler, steam and gas engine, and compressor operations.

Because of his rampant use of opioids, Marshall's body took longer to recover. Long past the stage of the immediate flu-like withdrawal symptoms, he still had the lingering sleeplessness and anxiety. Marshall used his downtime in the Power House to do push-ups to further strengthen his physique, and he drank copious amounts of water to keep his system flushed.

Although taunted by the other prisoners almost every day, in all his time at Mansfield, Marshall had only one fight. A guy named Scat, who had initially mocked Marshall in the cell block and who worked with him in the Power House, decided one day it was his turn to test Marshall's grit.

Part of Marshall's duty was to clean up the area at the end of his shift. He swept the floors clean and was mopping when Scat walked in and stepped on Marshall's newly cleaned floor.

"Man, why you walking on my clean floor?" Marshall said.

"N_____, who are you? You ain't nobody." Scat smirked.

Marshall was not looking for the fight he knew was coming. Neither was he afraid. "You didn't need to walk on that right after I mopped."

Scat sucker-punched him. Before Marshall could react, Scat's "travel companion," a boy from Cleveland, tried to pin Marshall's arms to his back. Marshall threw Scat's friend off into a black heap and grabbed Scat's shirt. He pulled him in close and said through clenched teeth, "You don't know who you're messing with, Scat." Marshall's rage resurrected, and he "beat last night's supper" out of Scat. He pummeled his stomach so hard Scat doubled over in pain and looked like he'd hurl. Marshall then landed one shot to the back of his head, and Scat fell to the floor, prone from the beating Marshall continued to inflict.

"Okay, n_____, I'm going to kill you."

Marshall grabbed a pipe from the floor and said, "I'm going to finish you. You're getting piped."

Scat's "boy" ran, screaming for help.

A contingent of guards streamed in, walkie-talkies crackling, and grabbed both men.

"Enough! Brandon, enough!" they yelled as two of them pulled Marshall off Scat. Sweaty and huffing, Marshall clenched his fists and glared at Scat, who pulled himself into a fetal position on the still-wet floor. One guard collected Scat like a sack of potatoes and dropped him onto his feet, his wobbly knees threatening to crumble again. The two guards who held Marshall respected his abilities and clenched his arms behind him.

Their quick tour through the prison halls at the hands of the guards made no detours, and their feet surfed above the concrete. They escorted Marshall and Scat straight to the hole—solitary confinement on D Block, two flights below ground floor and untold flights into a darker presence. Marshall winced with each of the three slammed steel doors, though the sound was not as sharp as on his arrival day. He heard a final slam as he entered the dark vacuum, which sealed him from light—from a way out. The guards deprived Marshall of his prison blues and left him clothed only in thin coveralls.

It was cold.

It was dark.

For three days, he languished in the below-ground squalor. No mattress adorned the hard steel platform next to a toilet he swore never saw detergent nor a brush, much less some light to reveal the filth. He thought a lot about who and what he was. In his heart he knew, he was—a killer. He realized his mortal nature to defend himself to the point of death, his or someone else's. He preferred it would not be his demise, so he always readied himself to do what he must. Each time he had the opportunity to commit the act, something external stopped him. This time it was the guards. Would that "something" stop him the next time? And he knew there would be a next time. He just didn't know when.

How do I avoid this again? How do I outsmart these guys? Do I have to kill Scat to get him to leave me alone?

No lights illumined the cell. No mail. No yard time. Aside from his thoughts, he and the other guys in the hole yelled out through the screens atop their separate doors. The guards meted out food through a narrow opening at the bottom of his cell door. Marshall ate it only to stay strong; it lacked any flavor.

Scat called out to Marshall, "Yo, Marshall, just tell them we were horsing around." Marshall wanted to tell Scat to shove it, but he had more interest in saving his own neck.

If I agree with him here, I can get out and take care of this guy.

After he thought it through, he played along and said, "Okay, man."

After three days in the dark, the men faced prison court before the captain of the guards, another guard, and a social worker. Marshall and Scat stood side-by-side, shackled together only in form. Marshall wished to be loosed from his assailant. He took the opportunity to lie his way out of further punishment and stuck to the script Scat suggested.

"Yessir, we were just messing around."

The captain of the guard looked at Scat's swollen eye and bruised and cut face.

"Is that the story you are sticking to?"

"Yessir, it happened just like Kali said. We was just messin'."

"Well, you and Brandon will be written up. No more fighting or you go back to solitary.

You both got that?"

Marshall nodded and agreed. Scat said, "Yessir. Yessir."

Ought to add "master" to that, Marshall thought as he swallowed the urge to sneer. The captain of the guards inclined his head to the retaining guard. "Take these prisoners back to their cells."

Marshall and Scat continued to work together in the Power House, and Scat did his best to extend an olive branch to Marshall. He'd learned his lesson about Kali: Don't mess with him. Marshall, ever wary, never turned his back on him or anyone else.

After Marshall was certified as a stationary engineer, he took advantage of the reforms enacted by then-governor James A. Rhodes. He attended the prison's Field High School, the first certified high school in an Ohio prison, and gained a legitimate high-school diploma. What he received while in Ft. Knox was a means to further opportunities, but it wasn't an official high-school diploma. He kept up the appearance of a good attitude and respected his authorities. They, in turn, rewarded him as an honor inmate. The fight with Scat marked his record, but other than that, his behavior and work record signified his desire to get out ASAP.

Prisoners generally take one of two approaches to their incarceration: negative, which means doing nothing to improve their lives, or positive, choosing to better themselves through the schooling and self-education opportunities offered by the state. Prison is a microcosm of society, with some inmates biding their time and/or getting in more trouble and some prisoners seeking to stay out of trouble and grow personally. Some even receive advanced educational degrees while inside. Marshall made sure he interacted with those of a positive mindset, and he vowed to improve himself and not let his situation get the better of him. He knew guys who got master's degrees through correspondence schools. He did his time; he didn't let time do him.

After Marshall completed his job at the Power House by getting his certification, he went to work in the on-site high school. He worked on their office staff as a clerk while he took his high-school classes. Marshall was part of the team that accepted inmates into the high-school program and was supervised by Mr. Mingus, the principal. A friend of Marshall's who was getting out connected Marshall with the principal, who also acted as their guard while they were in school. A gruff-looking Italian who smoked a cigar, his demeanor was winsome, and the men liked him. Mingus liked to "kick it" (laugh and joke) with the prisoners and called Marshall "Ralph" just to mess with him since he was going by the name Kali. Marshall chose not to confront him about that because he wanted to get along and get his schooling.

After he graduated from the prison's accredited high school, Marshall started taking classes through Ashland Theological Seminary, the only college curriculum offered at the prison. Classes encompassed history and science, and one of the professors came in one or more times a month and taught whoever was eligible and interested. Marshall was proud; he was the first in his family to attend college, albeit in prison.

This professor took an interest in certain inmates. By virtue of a bond issued by the warden, he arranged for them to leave the premises under his supervision. He even had some inmates at his house for a cookout, three or four guys at a time. A kind man to Marshall, his care for the inmates and the way he taught them led each toward success in their classes. He practiced a lifestyle of "love them till they ask you why."

Marshall's bond allowed him to leave the prison every day between 7 a.m. and 11 p.m., if a professor or other person with permission came and picked him up. Being outside, riding in a car as he stared back at the confines of the OSR made Marshall happy. The grounds of the OSR were not devoid of green grass, but its boundaries obstructed any vision of life outside the walls. Vistas of rolling hills and even farm country urged Marshall to press on toward release. That taste of freedom was a balm and an incentive for Marshall. Once he learned the system, he took great advantage of it, so he could get outside as often as possible. The only time the authorities refused him was when they deemed he needed rest.

He knew how to write a persuasive letter, and he sent many asking various schools and organizations to have him come speak. His motives served to get him out of prison on occasion (a day out) and gave him an opportunity to help others understand what prison life was like. The person in charge (professor, television or radio show host, or academic liaison) would follow the template Marshall sent, and their letters of request were generally accepted by the powers-that-be at Mansfield. His hot-button subject was predominantly prison reform, and he rarely got refused. Mansfield forged ahead of other places with its reforms and avenues of advancement in vocational and educational training, but Marshall knew of other prisons where inmates suffered abuse at the hands of their guards and superiors.

Ever an advocate for those who suffered injustice, Marshall wondered, *How can we make sure the public knows of the prison conditions that plague my locked-up brothers? What is our government doing? What is it* not *doing?* Reading history and seeing the truth, particularly as it affected Blacks, spurred him on to help others. Marshall believed in it and did not fear talking in front of groups of people. He garnered a lot of speaking engagements, and he further honed his oratorical abilities.

Marshall received invitations to speak at Oberlin College and other venues three or four times a week; there he developed friendly relationships with students and staff. He took some of the other guys from his group, and they had panel discussions with students and professors.

In addition to the inmates being able to go into Ohio schools and businesses for day trips, colleges often sent students, mostly those who majored in social work or criminal justice, to the OSR for on-site training. On one such occasion, Marshall saw a young woman who caught his eye—she floored him.

Man, I wish I could know that woman. She is fine.

Visions of her helped rekindle his fire to get out and better his life.

Even while trying to keep in line, Marshall at times would shout down his "better angels" and risk disobedience. Sometimes he engaged one of his brothers or a friend from Youngstown to write a bogus letter and get him out for a supposed speaking engagement. The letters they sent invited Marshall and his Black Culture Club to speak at a nearby church. One time the "church" engagement was an Aretha Franklin concert. Marshall would often drive his friend's car even though his license had been revoked since his incarceration. Once his boys flew out of the prison grounds, they rolled joints and smoked the whole day away. Marshall's vow not to get involved in drugs didn't include marijuana; to him, it wasn't a narcotic, simply a means to a buzz. He thought he could get away with it, and he did. He had worldly wisdom that didn't care about the stupidity of it. He wasn't thinking, *I'm a crook and a criminal.* He learned the system and felt he could do what he wanted, survive, and thrive.

Marshall set up events at colleges in northeast Ohio in conjunction with their Black History clubs to speak on prison reform or showcase prisoners who were artists and playwrights. The colleges' African American clubs, including the University of Akron (UA), also held art exhibits for the prisoners' works. Upon leaving an art exhibit at UA one day, Marshall spotted that same fine-looking Black woman he had seen at the OSR as she walked across campus.

I remember that woman. Oh, that woman's still fine.

His dream continued.

Upon their return to Mansfield, every inmate who had a day pass underwent a strip search. Marshall was no exception, and the guards didn't miss a crevice. Not once was he tested for drugs based on his countenance. They only did that when a guy wobbled or smelled of booze; Marshall always managed to air out on the ride back.

The food in the prison wasn't the best, and Marshall wanted to increase his nutritional intake, so he had some of the Oberlin students get him vitamins, which he carried back in.

Marshall entered the inspection area, thinking nothing of the supplements in his pocket. The guard found the packet as he searched Marshall. He held it up like a dirty diaper and summoned another guard. The two of them confronted Marshall.

"Brandon, what's this?"

Marshall protested, and the guard handcuffed him and marched him off to the prison hospital. Marshall didn't fight the guard because he felt he would be exonerated. No matter what he did when out on a day pass, he stayed within bounds while inside the confines of the OSR.

They shackled him to a bed, and under the watchful eye of the guard, the nurse drew blood to see what his blood count revealed.

Marshall thought, *Man, this is blown.*

"What are you doing to me? Hey, man, I didn't do anything wrong. Uncuff me."

"Brandon," warned the guard, "just sit there and shut up."

Memories of his mother's ubiquitous admonitions raised his hackles, but he was short. He didn't want to spend his remaining few weeks *in* prison *at* the prison, so he acquiesced. He lay back on the bed and held out his arm.

"Anything else?"

Marshall knew the blood test would reveal no drugs in his system, so he enjoyed his little rest on the infirmary bed. While the officials waited for the lab results, they placed Marshall in a holding cell away from his cell block. Even after the results came back as he expected, they kept him isolated from his normal routine.

While there, Marshall could still communicate with his boys and receive visits. He asked them to contact some Oberlin law students he had befriended. When the students made contact, Marshall said, "Drop by the warden's office the next time you come to visit me. Imply that you are thinking about a lawsuit."

They came to see him within a few days and did as he asked. The next day an unfettered Marshall had an escort to the warden's office.

"Where would you like to go, young man?" the supervisor asked.

Marshall's heart leapt; he knew he could write his "get out of jail" ticket right then and there. "What do you have to offer?"

"Parole," said the warden.

"Yes. I'd like that very much," he replied to the warden.

While Marshall entered prison as an addict at a low point, incarceration in many ways brought out good things in him. He became an honor inmate because he knew how to manipulate the system. His motivation was to get out, and while in prison, he worked hard, kept his nose clean inside, read a lot, and studied for his diplomas.

Marshall went before the parole board and was one of the first inmates released on the state's furlough program (instituted in the early seventies). Terms for his early release dictated he report to a halfway house for one year of supervision. Once he received word of his release, he told everybody at home he was getting out. All his old friends and family were waiting for him.

So were new temptations.

CHAPTER TWELVE

OUT BUT BOUND

After a quick process, Marshall packed and waited for word to go to the bullpen. He had given a lot of his stuff to other inmates, including his brother Watdell, who came in for drug possession and intent to distribute. Guards came and got Marshall, and they marched him through the visiting area to the outside.

Marshall's parole officer transported him straight to Akron. Marshall intended to enroll at Kent State, but Kent had no halfway house, so Marshall chose the University of Akron (UA). On January 3, 1973, Marshall was released from prison to Denton Halfway House in Akron, after fewer than three years in jail.

Marshall found Denton House on Furnace Street in a desolate section of Akron. It sat on the side of a hill and housed twelve parolees/probationers at a time. Because the area was so unpopulated, not much happened outside the mission house. As he entered and met the men who ran the home, he thought, *Who are these strange White folks? How do I survive here? I got to fit in with these people who are so different from me?*

At arrival, each man received linens, towels, and access to the laundry facilities. They got two meals a day and sometimes clothing, depending on donations from churches and individuals. Also, the premises held weight-lifting equipment, a ping-pong table, and a television. A man could leave the house at any time during the day, but curfew was 11 p.m., Sunday through

Thursday, and 1 a.m., Fridays and Saturdays. Residency was free unless a guy got a job; then he was expected to pay some rent. Rule breakers had to deal with their probation/parole officer and could go back into prison. Marshall took care to follow the rules.

I ain't going back to prison. No way, Marshall vowed.

The Reverend William Denton founded Denton House, and the residents called him Papa Denton. While the founder and supervisors were Christians, the men were not forced to adopt Christian beliefs. Papa Denton was an old evangelist in his late sixties or early seventies, and he preached the Gospel to prisoners in jails before it became popular. He also ministered to the down-and-out people in the Howard Street section of Akron, where a lot of men saw constant trouble.

What's the Gospel? Marshall wondered the first time he and Papa Denton spoke. He only knew the term in reference to some of the good music Aretha sang. He fell in with the rhythm, but the words didn't sink in. And when confronted by the Gospel, it didn't "take."

Papa Denton answered before any of the men could ask. When he ran into any of the guys, he told each about Jesus, who came to save all people from their sins. He was crucified in their place, so they could have eternal life in heaven with Him. Jesus died, yes, but He rose on the third day and is now seated at the right hand of His Father, making intercession for those who believe in and love Him. All it takes is admitting that Jesus is Lord, repenting of sin, and loving the Lord.

Marshall listened but didn't hear. All he knew was he made it out of hell, which he called 'Nam and the OSR. He recognized the goodness of the men who ran the place, but the *whys* of their actions didn't register. Posters and framed prints with Bible quotes hung throughout the common areas and in the rooms of the house, but Marshall paid them no mind.

Three of the largest churches in the Akron area began from that mission on Furnace Street. Marshall found himself surrounded by men of faith.

The motto, emblazoned on a board every man saw each day, was "Peace, Forgiveness, and Anticipation of a New Life."

Yeah, right. I'm a survivor, now, Marshall thought whenever he saw the sign.

He yearned for freedom. His mission—to be cordial and respectful and stay out of trouble so he wouldn't have to go back to jail. In his head, Marshall knew what he had to do and not do to stay out of the joint, but his heart persisted as an untamed entity—he never knew where it would lead him.

The in-house supervisor at Denton House was Dave Fair. Like Papa Denton, Dave treated all the men with respect. Available for talks or to give advice, Dave lived a godly life. One time he spoke into Marshall's twisted heart, "Marshall, do you understand what the peace of God is?"

"Man, I know peace. I got a woman," Marshall laughed.

"Marshall, do you have a relationship with Jesus Christ?"

"No, man, I don't. But I'm cool," Marshall said. Dave asked Marshall nothing else and Marshall went on about his business.

Once Marshall got established in Denton House and classes at UA, his family came over to visit. His brother Will drove his mom and Eva from Youngstown, and Marshall's mom and sister kept tabs on him through phone calls and visits as Marshall continued his parole. Still a young man at twenty-four, Marshall enrolled in the 1973 winter quarter at UA and majored in theater and mass-media communication. Bob Denton, Papa Denton's son, who trained to work for the mission house, taught his sociology class. Marshall's introduction to theater while in prison unearthed a talent he hadn't identified before except for the interest he showed when his cellie (cellmate), Larry, told Marshall about his vocation. Marshall loved playing roles and being onstage. Each weekday, he happily walked the twelve blocks to classes and reported back to Denton House every evening before curfew. He couldn't remember being so on track before, even in the Army.

However, the wheels were about to fly off the track.

———

Marshall had no idea how the guy found him, but a few months after getting out, a former inmate at Mansfield approached and offered him some heroin. Marshall thought, *What's one time?*

One time led him back into addiction.

He was had, again.

Out on furlough because he had been an honor inmate and in school to try to find a real purpose for his life, he landed back on drugs. Thus began Marshall's balancing act as a functioning dysfunctional man. Shades of his father.

He hung out on campus when not in class and one day saw the woman who caught his eye when she came to the OSR and again at UA campus on one of his days outside. As he watched her walk across campus, he got a longer look this time.

Man, she carries herself so well.

He asked around, found out her name was Katika Foster, discovered where she had classes, and made himself available.

In addition to majoring in social work, Katika played a role in the UA radio station as a well-versed DJ. One of his new friends from the radio station introduced them, and Marshall hung out while she DJed.

Marshall popped into the studio one day to see if Katika was on the air. When he saw her, he motioned a request to enter. She waved him in.

"Nice music you play," he said, trying to break any ice.

"Thanks. I do love music, jazz especially."

Marshall remembered what he had learned from Larry and asked, "Ever play any 'Trane?"

She raised her eyes and turned on the in-studio speaker. John Coltrane's version of "My Favorite Things" was playing at that moment. Pleased with himself and emboldened to continue, he reeled off many of the artists' names on her playlist before she had a chance to tell him who they were.

"Do you mind if I call you, *Tik?*"

Her smile melted his heart as she nodded her approval.

Ahhh, Marshall thought, *further inroads to her.*

The campus building that housed the radio station also contained the theater department, so while he hung out, Marshall met the students who ran the productions. He was around so much they asked him to audition for a part in Charles Gordone's 1969 play, *No Place to Be Somebody.* He won the lead role—a Black street guy named Johnny Williams who tended bar and pimped. *No Place to Be Somebody,* which originally won the 1970 Pulitzer Prize for drama, was billed as "A Black Comedy in Three Acts." *Time* magazine called it "A black panther of a play." It suited Marshall just fine. A play filled with drama, introspection, pathos, rage, mob mentality, inhumanity, ego, and murder was no small order to fill, yet Marshall cherished the experience. He felt like part of his own life had been written into a play. No, he wasn't a pimp, but the unfulfilled dreams of his character spoke into Marshall's soul. His character, Johnny Williams, also had a vision to become a Black militant. Marshall dug into the part full bore.

Would that he had absorbed the lessons taught by Johnny's bitter end.

UA took great pride in their productions, and Marshall got a bit of acclaim for his rendition. Tickets sold out every night, and Marshall had a lot of fun using his theatrical gift. It went right along with the acting skills he constantly employed to appear straight when on a heroin high. He went on to do several plays while in school, including one about Malcolm X.

During that same time, Marshall and Katika's relationship became more serious. Unusually shy, it took a while for him to ask her out. Fresh out of prison and making no money, he worried he had nothing of worth to offer her. He was ready to take her out on a date, and he had no pretenses. Their first date took place at McDonald's—he even got change back.

Marshall's heroin habit continued, his addiction following the usual pattern. The "friend" from Mansfield gave him enough free highs to get him strung out, and then he started paying for the drug. He naively thought he was strong enough to kick the habit whenever he wanted, but once he sank back into the mess, he lost the means to extricate himself.

Marshall finished his one-year furlough program in June 1974. He could leave Denton House but had to continue reporting to a parole officer. Marshall knew he skated but was too into the drugs to care. He thought he could overcome anything.

Despite all his bad decisions involving drugs, Marshall somehow got a front desk reception job at the Akron YMCA. He rented out rooms and answered and connected phone calls to the residents. After he left Denton House, Marshall tried a room at the Y, but its cramped condition made him uncomfortable, so he found a place with his cousin's girlfriend.

Word came to him through a friend that a better-paying job was available at the Phoenix Program, which served at-risk children who had been kicked out of school. After a little over a year, Marshall went to work for a program for at-risk children at the Akron Drug Abuse Clinic (ADAC). He took a job as a volunteer work coordinator until a better position could open up. They dispensed methadone, a drug that helps addicts get off heroin, but Marshall didn't take advantage of the drug, not even by stealing it.

Marshall lived two lives—he hid his addiction from the woman he loved, but he didn't hide his habit around like-minded friends. Friends? Only for convenience. He trusted none of them.

He asked for Katika's hand in marriage, but it took three times before she said yes. On their dates, Marshall would nod off from his frequent highs but passed it off as fatigue. He thought she couldn't read the signs of his addiction, and he was getting away with it. She knew about his prison past, but Marshall was such a good actor that he knew she had no idea he was hooked on heroin.

They moved in together in late summer 1974 and planned their wedding. Marshall had made enough money to buy a car from Dave Fair's brother, so he could drive Katika to Youngstown and show her where he grew up. She met his parents, and Marshall's mom liked her, never bringing up the other women from his past. Marshall was honest with his fiancée about everything but the drugs. She understood about the women he saw before her and even the children he had fathered, and Katika accepted him all the same. Marshall knew how to get on with people, and Katika's family liked him too.

Marshall and Katika married on September 30, 1974, at her mother's house.

Ruthie, Edward, and Eva came to the wedding. Katika wedded a man whose days began with *How do I get my high today, and how do I pay for it?* But for that hour in September, that day, they were happy together.

Marshall, generally high while working at ADAC, made a lot of drug deals on the job. He also falsified test results in exchange for drugs. Guys who were on the program had to produce urine samples for testing, and Marshall had clean urine available for their tests. Strung out and further out of touch with reality, Marshall missed a lot of work and eventually lost that job. He had a hunch they suspected him of using.

Knowing his addiction was overtaking him, yet powerless to change, Marshall worried he'd end up back in jail. Yet, he couldn't stop; he was incapable of making a good decision on his own. He lived in his own little world of doing drugs and faking responsibility. He loved Katika—that reality wouldn't change—and he worked hard to keep all his bad secrets from her. He didn't want his illusory balloon to burst.

Marshall and Katika shared a house with two other couples, the men had come out of Denton House. Each couple had responsibilities, such as buying food and cleaning, and utilities were shared. The couples had a dog so ugly they considered him cute—he turned out to be their much-needed comic relief. He resembled a Jack Russell terrier, covered with black-and-white spots, and above his pink nose, his eyes were always rimmed in red from allergies. Most likely, it was the constant pall of weed smoke that hung in the air. They named him after a character in *No Place to Be Somebody*, Mike Maffucci.

Food often disappeared from the kitchen table. Katika would make cookies and leave a plate of them out to cool, but before she could put them away, they often vanished. Butter left out for toast went missing; the plate looked like it had been washed. Everyone suspected one another of stealing their food, and things got tense until the day Mike Maffucci got busted. Katika caught him as he jumped up onto the table, looking for his next prize. His personality matched his namesake, a thief at heart.

Marshall followed suit and, since he had no job, started stealing things from the house to secure drug money. He lied and cheated. The drugs turned him into Dr. Jekyll and Mr. Hyde. He would never bring his drug friends around his wife, but they were his means of existence on the street. He didn't care about them but for what they could provide. While his wife worked, he hung with them. Often when Katika would go to their bank for money, there wouldn't be enough because Marshall had withdrawn it to get high. She asked him about it, but he always manufactured a lie to cover his tracks.

Marshall realized his wife was not fooled, and her trust in him eroded. He loved her, but his addiction trumped his emotions. Money continually came up short in their account, and one day she found Marshall's "book," the cubbyhole where he kept his needles and syringes. The long-overdue confrontation came when he got home that evening.

"Marshall, what's going on? What is this stuff?"

"Baby, I've got a habit," Marshall said as he sat there busted, disgusted at getting caught and not to be trusted.

"How long has this been going on?" Katika's tone turned compassionate, and she sat down next to her husband on their well-used sofa.

He made no pretense of his condition. Instead, he 'fessed up.

"I'm sorry. I've been using since I got out of jail. This guy got me addicted, and now I'm hooked." He left out the part about having been a user before prison.

"I want to support you. Get some help, and we'll get our marriage together," Katika said.

"I will support us while you go to rehab."

Marshall didn't recognize her grace, and he remained silent at first; he only knew he had been busted and needed a way out of the situation. He really didn't want to quit; his next words were only that—words, not promises.

"Okay, yeah, I'm going to get some help."

He knew the game. He acted his part in the play, not ready to get well. He thought maybe he'd get to the place where he'd say, *I give. I've had enough.* But in his heart, he knew that pipe dream of quitting would vanish. He knew Katika didn't know how that all worked, so he played her.

Marshall knew Katika thought he got help because she continued to encourage him. He also knew she watched the money and his actions closely because she didn't fully trust him. Still, he figured she had no idea that he had no intention to quit; the only thing he changed was taking more care to hide his addiction and his tools. He told her he looked for work but spent his time looking for drugs. He relied on money from their joint account, her money.

One evening in early summer 1976, when Marshall and Tik lounged in the house, talking, Marshall nodded off. By then, she read all the signs of his highs, and she finally had enough of Marshall's empty promises. She woke him, held his chin in her hands, locked eyes with him, and said, "I'm leaving you. I love you too much to watch you destroy yourself. Find yourself another place to live."

"Nah, that ain't happening, Baby." Marshall came out of his slumber. "I'm not going anywhere."

Katika threatened her husband only so long. Less than two weeks later, Marshall came home to their apartment as she packed the car with her belongings.

"Where are you going?"

Katika set a box in the car and stood to look at Marshall. "I told you I was leaving. I found somewhere else to live." Her job with the CETA program provided enough income for her to live on her own.

Marshall looked at her in disbelief. "How can you leave me with all this stuff going on?"

He didn't hear her, didn't believe her. "I lost my job. Now I got to lose you?"

Katika looked at him as if to say something, but instead, she got in her car and drove away.

She didn't look back. Marshall crumbled, kicked to the curb.

PART THREE

GETTING' CLEAN

CHAPTER THIRTEEN

UNRECOGNIZABLE

Katika took the only working car they owned. For the time being, Marshall stayed in the apartment and didn't know how he would keep paying rent without a job. She furnished and decorated the place; she represented the heart of their home. After she left, it became as desolate as his soul. He hated being there alone, but he had nowhere to go. He loved his wife, but he clung to his drugs.

The quiet in the apartment brutalized a socially needy person like Marshall, but it gave him time to think. He concerned himself with how to keep the place and procure drugs. A few friends offered some money, and some gave him a short supply of drugs, but only a few times because they were in as dire need of their highs too.

Marshall recalled a conversation with Jerry, a cancer survivor he met while he was employed at ADAC. Out of the experience, Jerry accepted Jesus and shared his faith with Marshall.

"Marshall," Jerry said, "coming through cancer was one thing I will never forget. But you know what? I would rather have died knowing Jesus than be cured of that disease and later dying without Him."

Oh, man. This is just like them Christians at Denton House.

Jerry knew Marshall's story and his situation with the drugs and Katika.

"Marshall, do you know what I think?" Jerry leaned in to make a point.

Marshall bent back as if that action would silence what Jerry had to say.

"You, my friend, are afraid of success. You keep getting sucked into an empty life because you want to. You have a lot to offer. Get out of the drugs, man."

Marshall just looked at him.

"Marshall, you are letting fear rule you. Fear is keeping you from succeeding."

With his wife gone and his house as dark as his soul, Marshall recalled Jerry's words and tried to consider what he might do to accomplish something, anything. But the drugs mastered him; they dulled his common sense.

That night, the tape of his childhood—the good parts and the abuse—played in his idle, drug-addled mind. He thought about what happened whenever things started to go well for him. He never consciously told himself, *I'm going to mess this up,* but his behavior inevitably caused him to fail. He couldn't break through the barrier of the abusive memories. He still heard in his mind his mother yelling, *"Shut up!"* and his father spitting out, *"Y'all are no good; won't be nothing."*

Marshall couldn't tell himself he could be a good man or a good husband. He didn't believe it; he didn't have those values on his own because of the way his childhood shaped his beliefs about himself. Katika provided enough boundaries at first to keep him at home, but her control only went so far. He always wanted to do more drugs and get higher than before, but while she inhabited the house, his respect for her, though shallow, held him somewhat in check.

With Katika's departure, so too went Marshall's will for a better life. The drugs claimed him and dictated his dependence. Marshall emptied himself into a hopeless life of more drugs, more women, and no parameters, except not to get caught and thrown back in jail. He loved Katika—she embodied everything he wanted in a wife. In essence, she was his god, but the drugs commanded his life. He found his hope in a syringe or a pill bottle, and his ongoing binge after his wife left started, in essence, a suicide run.

For safety, acquaintances allowed Marshall to camp out at their place. Sporadic girlfriends from here and there took care of him. The women he ran with prostituted themselves for him, giving him the money they made, money that allowed him to keep his place and buy more drugs. For a high, they sold their bodies. He became a pseudo-husband to one, in addition to pimping and whatever else he needed to do to survive on the street. He morphed into his own version of the character he played in *No Place to Be Somebody,* Johnny Williams incarnate.

Being high alleviated his desolation, but it wore at the very fabric of his being. He went wild in his grief at Katika leaving him. When he heard she was dating another guy, he wanted to hurt someone. However, his constant drug haze extinguished his fiery spirit, which now came only in fits and starts. His fists, too, lost their immediate clench response, as useless as his will. The drugs dulled his intellect, now trapped in a state of confusion and anger. The street drugs he did were suspect at best, not consistent in the high he expected. He couldn't count on the heroin he bought to be pure, and he knew if someone sold him bad stuff, he might kill the dealer. He decided to switch to prescription drugs, which would be pure and give a predictable high.

Marshall misused his innate talents to learn how to write scripts (prescriptions) for narcotic medications. He went to various doctors' offices to set up appointments, and when the secretary left the desk, Marshall tore off the bottom sheets of the prescription pad sitting near the phone. Since the sheets were numbered, pulling from the bottom allowed him more time to use them before the office personnel missed them.

He knew jail time might result from getting drugs illegally. The method he employed was monitored more closely, and his odds for success diminished with every false prescription. But so far, he'd worked the system successfully, just as he'd gotten away with falsifying the urine test results for clients as a drug counselor. Marshall didn't want to become too familiar with the pharmacists, so he sent one of his women to the counter to bust (redeem) the script as he hung back and watched.

His fall approached at full speed as Marshall scoped out another in a long string of drugstores. In his relentless search for emotion-desensitizing drugs, his memory had gotten so bad he couldn't keep track of where he had been. He and his latest woman, who turned tricks for him, walked into the drugstore, and she headed for the pharmacy counter to bust a script. She carried the money they made from their latest client, so they could pay for their drugs.

Marshall hung back and pulled the sleeves of his fatigues down to cover the tracks in his arms, even in the summer heat. He kept his hair relaxed, so it hung scraggly on his head under his hat. His beard was caked with sweat and food particles, and he noticed the clerks watch him as soon as he entered the store. Marshall loved sweet stuff, so he chose the candy aisle to watch the bust go down. The chocolate bars made him lose focus for a minute.

Oh, for a taste of sweet candy.

When he looked up, his woman was at the counter, fiddling with her purse to dig out the script. The female clerk looked up and caught Marshall's gaze. He looked away and walked further down the aisle, Milk Duds on his radar to make her think he was there for candy. When he looked up again, the clerk still squinted at him. As she shook her head and pressed her lips together, she turned to speak to the pharmacist, pointing at Marshall.

Uh oh, I'm blown.

As his woman stood at the pharmacy counter with the script in her hand, Marshall came up behind her and said, "Let's go—now."

Marshall and the woman left the store and got into the car. He dropped her off at her house and returned the borrowed car to his estranged wife, Katika. She still let him use her car for important tasks; this time, he told her he had a job interview. He left her place and walked back to his.

He walked around and up the back steps to the second-floor apartment, but before long, he heard someone on the front steps. A knock came seconds later. As Marshall opened the door, he saw his horrific past collide with his present. He recognized the top narcotics officer in Akron.

Just another White man comin' to hold authority over me. I am not *going back to jail.* "Marshall Brandon, we're coming into the house," the officer said after identifying himself.

"What do you want? You got a warrant?"

"No."

"Get outta my house!"

After the officer left, Marshall grabbed his hat and ran down the back steps and along the side streets to find a place to hide. He ran through alleyways and backyards to avoid any police who might still be in the street, then holed up in the back bedroom of some friends about two miles away.

Marshall heard what happened next from a neighbor. The police came back to his apartment and surrounded the house. Not finding him there, they went door-to-door looking for him, showing everyone a picture of the former felon, but no one gave him up.

Marshall evaded the police for a few months. He hid out during the day and ran the streets at night through that early fall. He found ways to feed his drug habit, pimping being the easiest route. That way, he could keep his high while avoiding pharmacies and doctors' offices where he'd previously stolen scripts.

A few months later, he thought the heat was off, and he and some of his boys tried to bust a new script. They didi'ed before they got anything and thought they got away clean, but the police cut them off within two blocks of the drugstore. Four cruisers surrounded them, and officers handcuffed Marshall and put him into the police wagon with his friends. He'd seen so many policemen through the years he knew the sheriff who oversaw the booking process.

Anxiety filled Marshall; he carried drugs and syringes in the roll-up hood portion of his army fatigues. The police made him strip and don the standard prisoner's orange jumpsuit, so he had to turn over his street clothes. For seven days, he sweated it out in the Summit County Jail, thinking they would find his stash.

But they didn't. His current woman bailed him out and he walked away from the jail after noon, looking like the wild man he was. He checked his fatigue hood, finding his stash still intact.

Back on the streets, homeless and strung out, Marshall wouldn't have broken a stick if he'd stepped on one. A solid 180 pounds when he got out of the Army, he now weighed about 130. Released on a nice autumn day, Marshall noted workers on the streets as they were going to and from lunch. As Marshall walked away from the jail that day, Katika passed by with a group of ladies and looked right past him.

"Katika!" Marshall yelled. "You're not going to speak to me?" He thought she ignored him on purpose.

She asked, "Where are you coming from? How you doing?"

"I just got out of jail."

She just kept walking. He figured she didn't want to have anything to do with him, and he was right.

I don't even recognize myself.

CHAPTER FOURTEEN

A NEW LIFE

Marshall knew the apartment provided no safety, so he shuffled back to his hovel of a room at his friend's and sank into the dirty mattress. And he prayed. *God, I don't know who You are. I don't know if You're up there.*

He claimed to be an atheist, but some of his friends professed Buddhism and others the Muslim faith.

If You're up there, God, which way do I go? Do I become a Buddhist or a Muslim? If You are real, show Yourself to me.

The friends he stayed with brought him some drugs, which temporarily bolstered his spirit. He knew what he wanted; he wanted his wife—his wife *and* drugs. He knew where she lived, so he went by a week or so after he saw her on the street. The first few visits consisted of small talk that turned into occasional meetups at her house, with Marshall asking for either money or use of the car. Their visits often ended in a fight. She talked about going to court and told Marshall, "I'm through with you. It's over."

Marshall lived in temporary housing not far from Katika. He thought about the woman he lived with; he didn't love her. He only used her for convenience, so he'd have someone to take care of him and a place to stay. Because he loved Katika, Marshall continued to go by and visit, but he rarely got his way. His mood bordered on belligerent and mean—despite his desire to win her back—which made her turn away and shut the door in his face. He no longer feared she would call the police, so he banged on her door until she came out to see him. She always told him when it was time to leave; she never knew which of his personalities would show up on any given day. Marshall always hassled her, though, whether high or not. One day, Katika chose not to buy any line he tried to sell.

"Marshall, you're not welcome anymore today. Please leave," Katika said.

"I'm not leaving. I'll leave when I'm ready to leave."

He often put his dog on when Katika told him it was time to go, and she threatened to call the police several times before. That day she'd had enough, and she did call the police to have him removed.

"Mr. Brandon, you need to leave," the officer told him. He had been called here before, and Marshall knew he couldn't get anything over on him.

"Okay, officer, thank you very much."

Marshall reluctantly left, knowing he'd try again, but he sensed Katika was, in truth, through with him. In his stubbornness, though, after a week or so, he went back to see this woman he loved and fully expected her to throw him out.

Marshall knocked.

"Hello, Marshall, come in," Katika said.

Surprised at her welcome, he cautiously followed her as she led him into the kitchen.

"What's up, Baby?"

He thought maybe she planned to butter him up, so she could present divorce papers. But she looked different—she exuded a peaceful countenance—and curiosity, caution, and hope filled him.

"Have a seat." She pointed to a chair at the kitchen table.

Marshall looked into her eyes and thought, *Wow! What is this?* "Marshall, our lives are not going to be like they were in the past." He narrowed his eyes and thought, *So, what else is new?*

He lost more hope. "What are you talking about?" he asked.

He looked at her and saw something that stirred up both curiosity and fear.

"I got saved," Katika said.

What the heck is "saved"? Marshall wondered. He heard about Jesus at the halfway house, but no one mentioned this term. At the same time, that something he saw in her was new. He immediately wanted some of what she had.

"I got saved, and I just want to let you know. Things *will* change in our lives. I want you to come and go to church with me sometime."

"Does getting saved have something to do with church?" he asked.

"Well, getting saved means you want to go to church, Marshall," she said. "I accepted Jesus as my Lord and Savior. That's what happened to me."

Marshall marveled at the difference in Katika but still didn't completely understand. Yet she wasn't kicking him out, a good thing. He'd expected to hear, "Don't come over here anymore. I want a divorce," and instead received a peace offering.

She now said, "I want to engage," and, "Why don't you come to church with me?" He thought about asking whoever was up there what he should do, but he let that thought just lie.

"I'll pick you up," Katika said.

Marshall wasn't losing this opportunity. "Okay, I'll go with you."

But he had no idea what this meant. He only wanted his woman back.

He thought, *The door's open; I'm going to get back. Ooooo, now's my opportunity to get back with Katika.* He was tired of being in the doghouse with her—he wanted out.

I'll jump, just tell me how high, he thought. Instead, he said, "When do you want to go?"

"I'll pick you up Wednesday evening."

Marshall didn't want to go; he feared what he might hear and see—who would see him. But he couldn't *not* go.

The next Wednesday evening, Katika picked up Marshall on a corner away from where he still shared a place with another woman. He didn't want his wife to see that woman. Katika didn't ask any questions as Marshall quickly got into her car. He knew almost nothing about church. He wasn't raised with any church-going agenda in his family. Vacation Bible school had been his only exposure to church when someone dragged him to it. He used the offering money his mom gave him to buy candy at the corner store instead. Other than that, he only knew Christianity through his Aunt Bessie and Uncle Henry, the men at Denton House, and Jerry.

Good people, but a little on the stiff side, Marshall thought as Katika drove to the church building.

When they arrived and walked in, he sensed a difference in the people, like they genuinely cared about one another. His world included the low-down and dirty—*get me drugs and keep me anesthetized whatever the cost.* He survived, but no one cared about him.

As they made their way past folks in this little storefront church in Akron, Marshall was quiet and respectful. He said hello and followed Katika's lead.

He discovered the people who greeted him were Christians who looked him in the eye; they didn't look down at him or his raggedy clothes. No one asked him for anything; they were kind and gracious. Marshall felt welcome and accepted. He felt kind of like he did when he went to Denton House. Only this time, he asked himself, *Who are these strange, Black folks?*

"How are you?" the pastor asked as he shook Marshall's hand. "Come on in."

Another man said, "Welcome tonight."

Marshall pulled his sleeves down before he shook their hands, so the men couldn't see the evidence of a lifestyle for which they would surely judge him—swollen hands and needle tracks. Hands like his were called "New York mitts," a term used for fighters whose hands swell from the ring.

He was comfortable but not, and when they were seated, he squirmed like a five-year-old until the service started. Then the goings-on held his rapt attention.

Since he knew so little about church, he watched so he'd know what to do to please his wife. *Hey,* he thought, *I'm an actor; I can fake this.*

The people sang some songs, and he thought the music sounded good. Though he wondered at what they did, he imitated what he saw. When they clapped, he clapped; when they said, "Amen!" he echoed them. He tried to sing the songs with them and show Katika that he was really engaged. But since he could never carry a tune, he sang quietly, not wanting to draw attention. But his thoughts didn't match his actions.

I'm a much better dancer; they should see me do the mashed potato. They'd yell "Amen" if they saw me dance!

In his heart, he knew he faked it all, but he didn't worry if others could see through his act. He thought he gave a star performance. When he and Katika left, Marshall realized he liked the people and the feeling he got while there. He never expected to like the experience, so he stayed quiet on the ride back. Katika dropped him off at the corner where she picked him up, while at his house, his other woman waited for him so they could get high.

Katika got in touch with Marshall before a week went by. "When are you going to church with me again?"

He went once more, but the next time she came to pick him up, he didn't. When they talked the next day, he lied and told her he had a meeting he couldn't get out of. He got high with his guys.

"Okay, next time. I'll pick you up Sunday, okay?"

He did go back again, but not every week. Each time he failed her, she let him off. She continued as patient and kind, and he questioned her constant tolerance of his behavior.

At first, he moved with halting acceptance into the "church thing" with her. But as he accompanied her more often, he began to get comfortable. He heard the Bible preached each time he went. While he didn't understand much, he felt a truth about it that nothing else had ever presented to him. He knew he had fewer smarts than others but didn't claim to be the dumbest guy either. He wanted to know about all of it, and he wanted to win back his wife, so he kept going back with her. But he continued to fake the funk. He stood and proclaimed, "Amen!" as he looked at Katika to gauge whether he impressed her.

Over a period of about four months, Marshall heard the preacher share the Gospel, that God sent His Son, Jesus Christ, to the world to save men. Yes, he heard the truth from other men, but this time differed. This time he listened with his head *and* his heart. He learned that whoever believed in God would not perish but have eternal life.

So that's what "saved" is, he thought. *But saved from what? Death? Hell?*

He skipped services but returned consistently, high or not. It came to the point where he looked forward to going with Katika, and she always picked him up.

Marshall's skepticism gradually turned to faith, and he believed what he heard. As his heart softened to the God he cried out to before, he started to loathe who he was at the recognition of his vile lifestyle. He learned that sin is anything that opposes God and His commandments. He learned he was a sinner—everyone was a sinner. But he struggled whenever the preacher made an altar call.

"If any of you wants to confess your sins and receive God's gift of salvation, come forward," the preacher said each week.

Marshall wanted to go forward several times. But in his mind, he kept hearing, *What are they going to think of you? You're a nobody. You don't belong here.*

He decided he needed to wait until he got himself together, cleaned up and out of the house and away from that other woman. Then he could get saved.

One day the pastor preached a message that included the quote, "Now is the day of salvation. Come as you are."

Marshall thought, *You mean I can come just the way I am? I don't have to wait until I am cleaned up?*

He scooted forward on the edge of his seat, waiting for the altar call.

At the end of the message, the pastor said, "Does anybody want to get saved or join the church?'

Marshall sprinted down the aisle, knocking off a few hats on the way. Smiles and amens followed him. Nothing held him back. All the past was just that, the past. All he knew was that he wanted Jesus. He wanted to be saved from the hell he had endured throughout his life.

C'mon now. Save me!

He knew in his heart Jesus is more important than anything else—the drugs, the women, even more important than Katika.

"What is it, brother?" the pastor said. "Do you want to join the church?"

"No, sir. Well, I don't know. I want to get saved. What's it take to get saved? I want to get saved!"

"Here, man, let me pray with you." The pastor grasped Marshall's hand and drew him into a side room.

Marshall eagerly followed the pastor. As the man bid him take a seat and bow his head, he heard the pastor say, "Lord God, we humbly come before You as needy people. Please bless this man with true understanding of what it means to be a child of the risen King. Give him clarity of Your voice as You lead him in salvation."

The pastor looked at Marshall and said, "Marshall, if in your heart you truly want to become a child of God, bow and pray with me. Repeat the words I say."

Marshall repeated the prayer of salvation and added his personal sins, "Oh, God, I am a sinner who needs Your grace. I have been abusive to You, to my life, and to my wife. I surely understand what abuse is. I am lost. I am a drug addict, and I need You to heal me. I believe Jesus came in the flesh and died for me." Marshall cried through the words and continued, "I believe He rose after three days and now sits at Your right hand. I ask You to make me clean and whole. Please forgive me of my many sins; I want a new life with You. Thank You for dying for me, so I can be Your child. Save me, Father God." Marshall looked up and saw his tears mirrored in the face of the pastor. And then he broke out in the smile of a child, a new creation in Christ—a child of Almighty God.

"Whoo!" he shouted. He knew Katika sat outside the room, listening and waiting for him to come out. He knew not only she but everyone else in the congregation heard him shout. He didn't care; he was forgiven!

"Marshall, welcome to the family of God," the pastor said, wrapping his arms around him. "What do you need? How do you want me to pray for you?"

Marshall was astounded. So full of joy he had no words, Marshall asked the pastor for just a minute so he could collect his thoughts.

He thought of all the wrongs that had been committed against him. He thought of how his mother would shut him up as he sniffled after a beating. He thought about how his tears this time were met with acceptance and love, not only from God but also from a pastor who led him in a prayer accepting Jesus and true life.

He also thought of the wrongs he committed against others, especially against his beloved wife. Wrongs that were now forgiven. *Hallelujah! I want to shout it out!* And he did.

"Hallelujah! What a Savior!"

With a heart that now beat with new life, Marshall looked at the pastor and said, "Pastor, please pray that I would be better with my wife. And I need a job—I don't even have a job." He looked down in shame as his tears ran off his face onto his shoes.

The pastor smiled and said, "Okay, we're going to pray for that."

Marshall, too buoyed to let his shame last, felt clean and whole. He finally got to dance in church because that night, he left cutting and sliding. He felt like he floated down the street to the car. Katika's arm in his was the only thing that kept him from soaring off into space.

Marshall and Katika got into their car, and he looked at her with new eyes, eyes that could now see the world that had been invisible to him for so long. From his childhood of abuse to his addiction and finally, to his abuse of his wife, his old life was unveiled to his eyes and, more importantly, to his heart.

He looked at his wife and cried. "Baby, I am so sorry for all I have done. I am sorry for the pain I've caused you, and I'm sorry for my sins against the Lord. Please forgive me."

Katika, as gracious as she ever had been, said, "Marshall, our lives will now truly never be the same. You have been called by the Lord to be His, and we will be His together. I forgive you; I forgave you the moment Jesus saved me. And now you understand the depth of God's love for us."

Marshall sat in his seat without speaking for a few minutes as Katika patiently waited.

"Tik, I have to tell you something."

"Yes, my love."

"I am clean. I have absolutely no compulsion for a drug of any kind. Tik, the Lord took my addiction away!"

It took everything in him to tell her that, not because he feared her but because of the awesome work of the Lord. Through fresh tears he said, "Tik, I'm so unworthy. I don't deserve to feel this way. I've led such an ugly life. How could Jesus just wipe my slate clean?"

He leaned into Tik's shoulder and let the tears that filled his eyes fall on her, cleansing them both with the knowledge that he joined her in being a new creation in Christ. He looked at his wife again and said, "You never gave up on me once you trusted Jesus as your Lord. I want to be worthy of your love. I am going to pray to the Lord to help me be the man I am supposed to be for Him, for you, and for the children I hope we have. I have so much to learn."

Marshall and Katika welcomed their new life in Christ.

Over the next few days and weeks, Marshall thought about the men God had put into his life, men he dismissed because he thought he knew it all. He thought of Papa Denton and Dave Fair, the man from Denton House who asked him if he knew Jesus. He thought of the professor from

Ashland Theological Seminary who had been so kind even as Marshall violated his trust.

Marshall thanked God for each of those men and the patience they had shown him.

He realized God protected him from far worse things that could have happened in his life. He thought of the days in Vietnam when he wanted to kill the CO who gave him extra duty. He thought of his militant leanings when he came back from Vietnam and how he wanted to kill "Whitey." He berated himself for turning to drugs when he could have turned to Jesus. But as soon as he thought that, he felt God nudging him, telling him that, in His time, God saved him from dying before he had the chance of salvation. And Marshall knew that God's timing is always perfect.

But I could have done so much for You, Lord, if only I had listened to the men you placed before me in Denton House. Shoot, even the time I had with that teacher from Ashland Seminary.

I sure have messed up, Lord. I didn't hear anything before.

And as if He were with him in person, God spoke to Marshall's heart, saying, "My son, I will use all that you have gone through for My glory. Just watch. If you let Me, I will do wonderful things through you."

On the way to Tik's the next day, Marshall went right back to the hood where his drug addict friends were, but not to do or sell drugs. He felt a great need to share what happened. He wanted to shout from the tops of the buildings that he knew Jesus.

Marshall—former addict, drug dealer, and pimp—was now an evangelist.

Indifference met him.

"Hey man, I got saved!" Marshall saw the same blank stare he knew he'd displayed when Tik first told him she got saved.

He repeated, "I got saved! I got saved! You've got to see this!" But his drug buddies weren't having any and didn't want to hear Marshall's testimony—his story of how he got saved and what it meant. Their reactions echoed the same.

"Get out of here, man. What you talkin'?"

"No, man, really. You've got to see this! I met Jesus."

"Man, get out. Get me some of them drugs you came here with the other day." Marshall thought they'd be happy for him, but the opposite was true, and he saw who he had been such a short while before. Struck down but not destroyed, he knew he'd be back to tell them what happened.

The old apartment he and Tik shared with their friends rented out to someone else long before. Once he ran from the cops, he didn't go near it again, and their friends abandoned it too. Even before he got saved, he didn't risk going after the security deposit for fear the landlord would lead the cops to him. No more jail for Marshall. He still resided with other friends, and he hoped Tik would invite him to once again live with her.

Heading back to her place, he smiled in anticipation of their future, even though he readied himself to confess what God had prompted him to tell her: all of his secrets.

He knocked on her door, not afraid anymore that she would turn him away. She invited him in.

"Marshall," she said, "where did you go?"

"Oh, Tik, I went down to see the guys to tell them about Jesus and how He saved me."

"And . . . ?"

"I think you know they rejected me," he said, "but I'll go back and share my story.

They've got to hear about Jesus!" Marshall continued, "Tik, to this day, I love my mom, even though her abuse changed me, and not for the better. I wanted so much for myself, and she took that away from me. I closed up. I shut down. Instead of speaking with this mouth the Lord gave me, I spoke with my fists to fight back at an enemy I didn't understand. And now—now I want to shout to the world how good God is. It's as if He brought me back from the dead. I can speak now. I can share His story with anyone within hollerin' distance." Marshall chuckled and said, "I know the Lord has things for me to do. I only hope He gives me the time and opportunities to speak. I can't sit still, all wrapped up in myself anymore."

Tik leaned in and pressed her forehead to his. "Marshall, I believe God has plans for you too."

He braced himself for his confession to her. "Tik, I've been staying with a woman. I don't love her. I love you. I'd like to come and live with you. Will you let me come stay with you until I get back on my feet and get a job, so I can get out of this situation? I don't need to be there with that woman; I need to be here with you."

"Yes, Marshall, you can come." She didn't hesitate, not one bit.

And he never wanted to leave—once he got his feet back in the door, nothing and no one was going to push him out. Within two weeks, Marshall had a job, albeit a temporary one, through the CETA program in Akron (a government-sponsored employment training/access program). Soon after, he started working for the Akron City Water Department, and all the while, he grew as a Christian.

Every time that little church opened its doors, Marshall showed up. He totally separated from the friends he had before he got saved, mostly because he didn't want to get reinfected with the lifestyle. A Christian is called to interact with unbelievers, but he knew his faith needed to grow. His acts of service for the church included cleaning and washing toilets at the church building. He'd go each Saturday and run the sweeper in preparation for the Sunday service. Marshall radiated happiness.

He repeatedly marveled at how God had delivered him on the spot from his drug addiction. He never again used after that night, and he realized the miracle because he had no taste at all for drugs of any kind. Before that moment, in addition to anything he could shoot up, he had been using speed. His weight, which had taken a slight upturn after being in jail, plummeted back to 130 pounds. He didn't have to think about or will himself to try to quit drugs; the compulsion left as if he'd never had it.

Within six months, Marshall and Katika moved into a new apartment, and within a year, they talked about starting a family. Even though she had forgiven him, Marshall knew he had to win back Tik's full trust. He wanted it to be as immediate as the delivery from addiction, but, in fact, he knew it would take time, maybe years, for her to fully trust him. He knew God helped him grow into a man of integrity, so he had to display the fruit of the Holy Spirit that now ruled his life every day as he matured as a Christian man and husband.

He demonstrated how she could trust him with money by not stealing a penny or lying about anything. The microscope under which he knew she had him was a discipline he welcomed. Over time she finally began to take him at his word, and in some ways, she started to take her foot off his neck.

He thought, *Okay, with God's timing, hopefully, she'll fully trust me soon.* And the healing came, along with renewed and rewarded trust.

Marshall also had other people to whom he was accountable: in-laws who knew his history. Because he had been abusive to Katika with his deception, he knew her family also looked at him with mistrust. He knew they wanted to protect her. His MO had been aggression and winning the fight at any cost. His past behavior toward Katika was restrained compared to how he dealt with others. At the time, she was unaware of the depths of his depravity and his proclivity for violence.

But abuse is abuse, and any amount is too much, and too much transpired in his history with his wife. She'd begun to trust him again, but he had to win the trust of her family too. He'd made the decision; he knew Jesus, and he knew his heart was new. He swore he would never raise his fists in anger again. Nor would he continue using the foul language he had so easily learned and carried with him from childhood. To think of the language that was recently normal for him made him cringe. He told Tik's family they could trust him, and they learned to do that.

Katika got pregnant in 1979, two years after he got saved. They discovered they were to have a son. They prayed for their boy to be healthy and dedicated him to the Lord while he still grew in her womb. This was a big step for Marshall because he still had to learn what being a father meant. It took him so long to get over himself and his past sins and mistakes he sometimes faltered as he considered giving over his son to God.

As he and Katika went through the process of thinking, praying, and then getting pregnant, Marshall thought a lot about the ones he "left behind." He was convicted about paying his son, Keith, no attention at all. After his redemption, when he confessed everything to Katika, he didn't leave anything out, including the two children he had fathered. Together they decided to do all they could to restore a loving, welcoming relationship with them. It was a big step for both because they had to fully trust God for the outcome. Marshall knew how to locate Keith, but Kendra had given their daughter up for adoption, so he had no idea how to find her.

Marshall had been in touch with Joyce and Keith because Ruthie maintained a relationship with them. They all lived in the Youngstown area, only an hour away. He saw Keith several times over the years since he was born, but their relationship hadn't grown. When Keith was in his early teens and before Marshall and Tik were expecting, he asked Marshall if he could come over and spend some time with them. Tik was instantly agreeable, and he stayed a week with them that summer.

After a few summers, Keith asked Marshall if he could come live with them. In addition to the desire of responsible, godly fatherhood, Marshall worried about Keith's home environment. Joyce had four other children by other men, and they lived in the projects of Youngstown, where many drug deals went down. The subsidized housing, home to many poverty-stricken people, reeked of drugs and hopelessness.

Marshall asked Katika, and she agreed to invite Keith to move in. Before he told Keith, however, Marshall spoke to Joyce to gain her permission. He kept Keith in the loop and told him he had to ask his mother for her permission and formal release. Joyce granted her approval, and Marshall and Katika completed all the necessary paperwork and processes necessary to adopt Keith as their own.

During that process, Marshall and Tik's first child, their son Kali, was born in June 1980. Marshall's life changed again, for this great moment exponentially widened and defined his journey to become a man of God.

Wow, God has given us a son, as well as Keith, Marshall thought, *I need to step it up and make sure my family is well cared for. O, Lord, I sure do need Your help with all of this.* Marshall prayed this prayer more than once over the next few years as his new son and his relationship with Keith grew.

He considered it a privilege to have not only one but two sons, and he basked in the joy of a restored relationship with his wife. But he wondered how he could raise his sons and teach them in a way that differed from his own upbringing. *How am I going to teach them to throw a ball or change a tire, or even fish? No one ever taught me. I can do these things, but how do I teach my sons to do them?*

Marshall knew no parental role models he wanted to emulate. He didn't receive the gift of a relatable role model from his "absent" father, so he started from scratch. Marshall took on the process of learning what other men do by watching and questioning the Christian men in his church.

Keith came to live with them in 1982, after they moved to another area in Akron when Kali was two. By then, a sixteen-year-old Keith enrolled as a sophomore in Firestone High School. It baffled Marshall and Katika that Keith had been placed in the "slow" classes in Youngstown because he displayed intellectual competence. They had him tested, and, indeed, Keith demonstrated a solid IQ. Katika helped him assimilate into their family and church. He was a good young man, compliant, trouble-free at home, in school, and in church. He completed his schooling in regular classes.

They taught Keith the advantages of a Christian household. Though he once tried to get out of going to church by faking a headache, Marshall called him on it and said, "In this household, we attend church." They all rejoiced when Keith asked Christ into his heart about a year or so after moving in with Marshall, Tik, and Kali.

Marshall forgave his parents and brothers, and he told them what Jesus had done for his life. He shared the Gospel with them every chance he got, but at that time, none of them wanted to change. That didn't hinder Marshall and Katika's prayers for them.

Marshall continued to learn and grow as a husband and father as he sought wisdom among the men in his church. *Hmm,* he thought, *God put these men in my life for a reason.* As he talked to the other men, he learned that some of them weren't too good at their parental and spousal roles either. But they prayed together and learned from the wiser men, and they grew into good husbands and fathers.

But more trials approached.

CHAPTER FIFTEEN

ATTACKS

While still working for CETA, one of Marshall's old habits persisted: smoking. He knew he needed to quit but had a hard time doing so. One time when he drove down the street, cigarette in hand, he saw his pastor approach from the opposite direction. He hid the cigarette, so his pastor wouldn't see it. Immediately, the Spirit convicted him both of smoking and hiding it from his pastor to keep up proper appearances. About a year into his new faith, one of the last things he wanted to do was walk into church smelling like a cigarette, so he asked God to help him with it. When someone becomes a Christian, the Holy Spirit becomes part of him and helps guide him (or her). Marshall now knew and reacted to the difference between right and wrong.

Marshall prayed the night after he saw his pastor on the road, *God, please help me quit smoking.* God, as Marshall says, "got busy" the next morning and answered that request. When Marshall arrived at work and lit up, he got sick as a dog, like never before. He looked up and said, "Eeeew, I get it, God." He threw the offending cigarette down and stomped it out. He gave the remaining pack to Ron, a coworker and friend he knew at Denton House, and said, "I'm done." He breathed a clean sigh of relief and thought, *That's another addiction I'll never worry about again.*

Back in the day, Ron and Marshall used to get high and chase women together. Ron still egged Marshall on to smoke weed with him, which Marshall had staunchly refused since becoming a Christian.

"What's up, Kali?" Ron used Marshall's prison name. He couldn't—or wouldn't—understand the change in Marshall. And he sure didn't seem to get why Marshall handed over a pack of cigarettes. "Who do you think you are?"

"I'm saved now," Marshall said. "I'm changed, and God is in my life. I'm a young Christian, and I'm trying to do the best I can. Smoking is something I can't do anymore—don't want to do anymore."

Ron spat at Marshall, jumped on him, and bit him. Marshall tried to wrest himself from Ron's grasp. As a young Christian, the assault from his old buddy caught him off guard. Confrontation with his past sin mortified him—that it came from a friend he thought he knew and could trust.

Ron's anger rose, and he pulled a knife on Marshall. "I'm going to cut you, man."

Marshall's irritation rocketed and got just as ugly, one thing he still carried from his life before Christ. "Don't make me kill you, Ron." Marshall grabbed his neck and knew he almost killed him because, as Ron flailed and sputtered, his face turned as ashen as a Black man's could. Marshall knew immediately he had slipped back into his old self. He silently prayed for God to pull him out of the rage of his previous life, and with God's help—for that moment—he stopped.

Ron sat up and Marshall tried to apologize.

"Oh, man. I am sorry, Ron. Please forgive me."

"Just stay away from me," Ron said. "You and your God, you just stay away from me."

Marshall went home that night and told Tik about Ron. He showed her the bite marks.

"Marshall, you know what that was, don't you?"

"Yeah, crazy Ron," Marshall said. "He wanted to kill me, Tik, just because I wouldn't smoke weed or cigarettes with him."

"No, Marshall, the devil used Ron to try to get you back into his fold. He always hates losing someone to the Lord. He wants you to be evil again, and he used Ron to attack you."

"Really?" Marshall said. "Man, I thought those days were over, me fighting people off.

Now I got to fight the devil?"

"Yes, but the Bible tells us greater is He who is in you than he who is in the world.

The devil can't have you anymore, and he wants to cause you to stumble in your witness for Christ."

"Well," Marshall said, "I plan to give him one heck of a fight because I know the end.

We win! Hallelujah!"

This conversation took place just before supper, so as the meal (and Kali, their son) waited, Marshall and Katika bowed their heads in prayer and thanked the Lord for His help. They smiled and hugged and ate their meal while they talked about all the other happenings of their day. Marshall shared another victory.

"And something else, Tik. The Lord took away my nicotine addiction. I prayed last night, and He took it away today. Man, this is some God we serve."

Tik smiled again and shook her head in wonder. "You know, Marshall, I'm never surprised by what God can do, but I always stand amazed."

Marshall recognized the Lord's work on his growth. The release from smoking delivered almost as great a miracle as his freedom from drug addiction, another defining victory in his life. He learned that day the devil's attacks seem to be the most insidious after a moral and spiritual victory. He knew he had to cover himself and be covered by others with prayer.

Marshall's temp job with CETA lasted only so long, and he started to consider using the stationary engineer certification he received in Mansfield. At the time, he had seen it only as a path out of prison; now he realized it could be a means for a living, a way to take care of his growing family. *How kind of God to let me use something from my life in prison. Wow, He redeemed my time.*

As he looked further into using his certification, Marshall found out his mother kept his license renewed. Each year the state sent a notice to him in care of his mother's address, and she kept it up to date.

He called her and said, "Praise God, Mama, thank you for doing this for me."

She said, "Somehow, I knew that license wouldn't be wasted. I am so glad you can use it." She said nothing about his praise to God.

Marshall heard about a job opening at Ohio Edison energy plant that required his type of license. He prayed about it and had others praying for him to get the job. His pastor, who knew his past, wrote a letter of recommendation for him. He got an interview with a supervisor, whom he was about to discover was a brother in Christ.

"Are you a Christian?" the supervisor asked Marshall during the interview as he read the letter from Marshall's pastor. Marshall knew this had nothing to do with the job interview but didn't mind that he asked.

"Yes, I am."

"Well, praise the Lord, so am I." Their conversation turned to spiritual matters. They talked about God and "had church" right in his office as they prayed and worshiped the Lord together.

Marshall thought, *Another man the Lord has sent to show me He is here with me.* "Listen," the supervisor said as he looked over the first page of Marshall's application,

"I tell you what. I don't make the final decision. I screen the applicants and make recommendations based on experience and the job description." And then he looked more closely at Marshall's paperwork. "You have a license?"

"Yessir, I do."

"Why don't we leave this up to God?"

"Sir, that's the only way I want to go," said a beaming Marshall. "If God is not in it, I don't want it."

Marshall went home that night full of expectation and only a little doubt. "Lord," he prayed, "I give this all to You. You have made Yourself so real to me, and I bow to the plans You have made for my life. It's all about You. But if it's okay with You, I'd really like this job, so I can support my family."

The next day, while at home, Marshall leaped from the couch when the phone rang.

"Mr. Brandon . . ."

Has anyone ever called me Mr. Brandon out of respect? I sure hope this is a good call." . . . this is the Ohio Edison plant calling. Can you come to an interview tomorrow at the Gorge Power Plant in Cuyahoga Falls?"

Marshall wanted to scream in delight, but he held his emotions in check. "Yes, sir, I certainly can. I will see you then."

The interview went well, short and sweet. Marshall knew God had His hand in it when the supervisor said, "Mr. Brandon, you can start whenever you want."

He wanted to start right away, but he did what he thought to be the honorable thing. He asked if he could work out a two-week notice at the job he still held. They graciously granted him that option, but when the time came for him to start, Ohio Edison began its first strike ever. With a family to support, he didn't need unemployment. His bosses at the energy company assured him he would be brought on board as soon as they settled the strike.

He prayed and asked God to help him in the interim, and Marshall found a temporary job at the Salem Potato Chip factory. He marveled at how he could save money and pay bills instead of using all he could get to buy drugs. A new adventure of God's provision awaited him every day. He had not one bit of regret about his decision to ask Jesus to be the Lord of his life. Now a happy man, his relationship with his wife grew more and more precious in its mutual trust and respect. Marshall knew God could open any door He wanted. He needed to walk by faith and tried as best he could.

In October 1978, after three months, the Ohio Edison strike ended, and Marshall finally started his new career. The Gorge Power Plant sat on the Cuyahoga River between Akron and Cuyahoga Falls. Built in the early twentieth century, the facility originally burned coal to provide power to trolley cars. Later operated by Ohio Edison, it produced power for sections of Akron. Marshall enjoyed the work, but he soon realized living out his newfound faith in the workplace would not always be easy.

Christianity is like a bolt of cloth with many folds. Many denominations agree on the nonnegotiables of the faith. (Jesus is Lord. He died on the cross to save humanity from their sins, therefore offering salvation to all who believe in Him and proclaim Him as Lord. He rose after three days in the grave and is now in heaven interceding for the saints, who are all the saved. Communion and baptism are ordinances of the faith, with both being symbols of one's declaration of Jesus as their Lord, etc.) Some denominations differ in distinctives (how *often* to partake of communion and baptism, etc.).

It didn't take long for another coworker to confront Marshall about his faith. Just as the attack by Ron, evil parlayed its chance to assault Marshall on a different front. He looked forward to discovering Christian coworkers and didn't realize not all Christians thought alike. One of Marshall's new coworkers claimed faith in Christ but as part of a different denomination, and he asked Marshall about the assurance of his salvation.

"Have you spoken in tongues?" the coworker said. "How do you know you have the Holy Spirit?"

Marshall fought the battle inside with all his heart. Still growing in his faith, he didn't possess all the answers needed to defend himself to the man. He grappled with how to answer him with love and patience.

"Yeah, I'm saved. No, I do not speak in tongues, but I know I have the Spirit within me. I know, because I know because I know. He took away my addiction; that's one way I know!" Far from a theologian at this point, he still knew God had delivered him.

His coworker, however, was relentless.

———

The coworker pushed his version of the Bible at Marshall, along with his contextual assertions, and Marshall started down the path of doubt. *Do I need to do that? Am I supposed to speak in tongues? God, I want to know exactly what I am supposed to do.*

He answered his coworker, "Oh, man, I don't even know the answers to what you are saying."

Marshall didn't concede to him. Instead, in his evenings at home, he dug deep into God's Word, the Bible, and asked Him to reveal the answers to his questions. *God, show me.*

The Lord led him to Scripture passages about the assurance of salvation and the gifts of the Spirit. Marshall also asked his pastor and other more mature Christians, and they helped him understand.

Marshall knew God spoke to him through His Word and through his fellow Christians, and he learned how to answer his coworker. He used the diplomacy God gave him and said, "This is what God's Word says. Don't add to that. I know what I needed, and that was and is a relationship with Jesus. I now have that, and I am forever saved. I now have everything I need."

Marshall wanted to grow, and God used that confrontation to lead Marshall into a habitual study of the Bible. He loved it! He became an example of a good Christian man in his workplace by walking his faith; he lived what he believed. He did not become self-righteous, so he ministered as a man who came from the streets, and he never forgot what that was like. The coworker who confronted Marshall had been a Christian for several years and came across as self-righteous and legalistic. He held staunchly to his assumptions and would not grow past his own immaturity.

Marshall noticed that the man had few relationships with others at their workplace. To Marshall, the man seemed to have his nose stuck in the air, saying, "I have something you guys don't. I'm sanctified, born again, baptized with the Spirit, and I speak in tongues. You don't, so I'm better than you—closer to God."

Marshall carried himself as a Christian man who related to others, no matter who they were. Being on the street for so long gave him an "in" with the other guys, and he was far from sanctimonious. They respected how he came from the streets yet made a better life for himself. Humble and relatable, Marshall gained quite a few new friends and their trust at the power plant. He shared his faith with some of the men, and he walked away from groups of men who occasionally had porn magazines.

"What's the matter, Marshall? You can't look at this, can you?" one asked him.

"Oh yeah, I am free to look at all of that," Marshall said. What he thought was, *You have to because your daddy, the devil, tells you to.* What he said was, "I've got a choice now. I can look at it, or I can walk away. I choose to walk away because I have freedom to."

God gave him the chance to talk with them, not in a condemning way but in a way that showed patience and love. He faithfully read and followed the Word every day. He picked up a book about reading through the Bible, and God gave him numerous opportunities to share how God redeemed his life and about being saved.

One day he shared news about his new Bible with several guys at work and how he planned to read through it each year. One of the guys named Lenny became a Christian after Marshall shared his faith with him. Eventually, ten men at the Gorge Power Plant gave their hearts to the Lord because of Marshall's witness.

Marshall had been a burden to his family for much of his early life, especially his mother, so he started sharing the Gospel more with her. She had once been a churchgoer and sang in the choir when young, but she had long periods where she didn't go at all. At fifty-nine, she was diagnosed with cancer, and as he and Katika visited her, they asked her if she knew Jesus as Lord and Savior. "Mom, do you know Jesus? Are you saved?"

"Yes, I am, Son," she said.

Marshall was floored. He had so many questions about why she treated her family so poorly, but he knew now was not the time to bring any of that up for discussion. But she gave Marshall such assurance with what and how she told him, he believed he would indeed see her again in heaven. When she died from the disease, they celebrated her life instead of grieving a soul lost forever.

Edward passed away two years after Ruthie. Marshall and his dad had been able to spend good time together after Ruthie passed, and Marshall even recognized glimpses of sobriety. When his father was on his deathbed, Marshall asked him once again if he knew the Lord Jesus. He didn't, so Marshall led him in the prayer of salvation just hours before he died.

Lord, thank You for saving my parents. Thank You that I will see them again in glory. Marshall met regularly with his pastor. One day the pastor said, "Marshall, you need to tell your story to folks. You ever think about going into jails to share?"

"No, but it sounds like just the thing I need to do," Marshall said.

Marshall's pastor knew many people at the jails, and he connected Marshall with those who could get him access. Marshall began visiting local jails every Friday and sharing his testimony. From those times came the opportunity for him to go into penitentiaries all over Ohio. Katika also got involved in local-prison outreaches as Marshall continued to share the Gospel all over the state.

A prison ministry team formed at their church. As they went into the jails, they led a time of worship, and then Marshall and other team members shared their testimonies. Men and women got saved by the busload. Marshall found a calling.

After Marshall's salvation, his home church enjoyed a few more years in their storefront location. Then, because the congregation kept growing, they made two location moves before the pastor had a vision to build a new facility.

Once in their new building, one of the first ministries they started involved theater, something right in Marshall's wheelhouse. He directed a play called *The People vs. Jesus,* a profound drama the church used as an evangelism tool. The audience was the jury, and at the end of the play, they had to decide: Was Jesus guilty of fraud by proclaiming to be the Son of God and Savior of the world? The audience (the jury) delivered a verdict of life or death for the Accused. As the prosecutor called witnesses (John the Apostle, Mary Magdalene, James the brother of Jesus, Herod the Tetrarch, and Mary, the mother of Jesus), they gave testimony about their time with Jesus of Nazareth. God used the play, and many people came to faith through the performance. People packed the place, so they decided to continue producing it on an annual basis.

As the congregation grew, so did Marshall. Discipled by his pastor and other godly men in his church, he eventually taught Bible studies and occasionally preached. As he grew, he ran into men he knew from back in the day.

Michael P. was one such man, and Marshall repeatedly saw him in prison as he went in to minister to the inmates. The two of them previously shot dope together, and Marshall learned that Michael had been in and out of prison for many years. He kept getting caught.

Marshall went with the prison ministry team to visit Michael. "Mike, you back again?"

"Man, I'm trying."

"Quit trying and start trusting. Your trying's not going to get you out. You've got to trust God."

Michael soon gave his heart to Christ. When he got out of prison, he started a ministry, helping men as he had been helped.

Marshall met a woman named Delia, who served time for prostitution. A heroin addict who lived in an area where Marshall and Tik once lived, Marshall's testimony led her to the Lord, and she gave her heart to Jesus.

She told Marshall, "I just want to tell you, Marshall, Jesus is so good. I am doing so good!"

Delia's daughter was also an addict, but because of how God used Marshall, Delia's daughter got saved and finished her schooling.

Marshall saw fruit from his labors for the Lord. When not working at the power plant, he did his prison ministry. Eventually, he started a bus ministry where once a week, he borrowed a bus from the church and transported families to prisons to visit their loved ones. To Marshall, being at church for eight hours on a Sunday was nothing. He loved the change in his environment and adored being around God's family, the church. God indeed had taken him from darkness to pure light.

Yet darkness would again try to steal his joy.

CHAPTER SIXTEEN

NOW, LORD?

Amid his spiritual growth, Marshall felt a call from the Lord to go into pastoral ministry. But his initial response was to think, *I can never be a pastor. I can't do that.*

He allowed his past to dictate his future. Prison ministry was one thing; he'd been in prison, so he knew he could speak to prisoners. Yet, he resisted the call to become a pastor because of his background of family dysfunction, abuse, and drug addiction. He didn't feel worthy of this calling.

Lord, I can't do this; I'm a bad guy—a street guy. Me? Please ask somebody else. Marshall wrestled with God about this call to a new purpose. The prompting of the Holy Spirit convicted him, and he continued to pray about it and declare his unworthiness for such a high calling.

His church leaders introduced Marshall to an in-depth Bible study, called *Equipping the Saints,* which provided the equivalent of two years of seminary training. The study consisted of four books, each of which took sixteen weeks to complete and covered everything from the foundations of the faith to discipleship. As he began to dig into this new study, Marshall grew in a different way—he learned theology that undergirded his new relational character. In the process, Marshall trusted more people because of Spirit-given wisdom. Without that, Marshall would have relied on his past and his own devices. He couldn't trust people in his former life, but this new territory encouraged him.

Wow, he thought, *God has even given me a group of people I can rely on. I don't deserve this, but I'm not refusing it either!*

Part of his training included Scripture memorization, and he marveled that learning lines for plays had *nothing* on the studying and memorization of passages from the Bible. Marshall memorized verses that addressed assurance of salvation, prayer, how to have quiet time with the Lord, Bible study discipline, how to teach a Bible study, and how to share your faith, along with many other foundational principles necessary for church leadership.

In 1984, the Brandons experienced two special blessings. They had a daughter, Imani, in September, and Marshall finally quit fighting the call to be a pastor and said yes to the Lord. *Yes, okay, I give. If You want me to be Your minister, I'll do it. You just tell me when.* Excited at the outset, he wondered, *Okay, where is God going to send me? How are You going to do this, Lord?*

Marshall shared his calling with Katika from the start, and after he said yes, he told others. One of those was Lenny, the man with whom Marshall shared his Bible reading plan. Lenny began telling everyone about Marshall's call into the ministry. But Marshall chuckled as he said, "Lenny, share your own testimony. Let me share mine."

As Marshall anticipated an opening for a ministry position, the Lord said, "Wait."

So, he waited through the rest of 1984 . . . 1985 . . . 1986 . . . .

As he waited, Marshall continued to work for Ohio Edison, but no ministry doors opened for him. He served his employer well as a good employee, a hard worker who came early and stayed late when needed. He helped other employees and tried to be a good Christian witness to them. Though, as he waited, his heart's desire switched from his job and more toward the longing for a leadership role in ministry. He grumbled his disappointment and anger to the Lord. *Okay, God. You said You were going to call me into ministry. Where is it? What's up with this?*

One day during that period of waiting, he listened to WCRF, the local Christian broadcasting arm of Moody Bible Institute. He heard Pastor Warren Wiersbe's message titled "Bloom Where You Are Planted." The message spoke directly to Marshall's heart, and it resonated within him.

Okay, God, I got it! I just need to bloom where You planted me. I am already doing ministry, and right now, You have planted me here at work, so I need to be faithful right where I am. I'll be the best Christian I can where I am.

Marshall's perception changed with that realization, and he walked back into his job with a new determination to be the man God created him to be while God prepared him for what came next. As his faith grew, so did his trust in God, and his renewed heart exhibited his faith, trust, and love in a way he hadn't shown publicly before. He wasn't afraid to open his home to church groups, and he opened his heart to other godly men without fear of condemnation.

He began to realize God's perfect timing for his future stretched far above his expectations. He found he finally trusted God with the timing of his calling to ministry and knew He would exceed Marshall's expectations at the right time. As a result of this new trust in God for his future, he discovered he loved his job and thought, *I would like to retire from this job.*

Marshall saw lives and families changed. He became a deacon within his church body, and his pastoral leadership skills matured. A deacon helps the congregation by serving and even teaching, and he appreciated such a fruitful ministry.

In 1988 Marshall started a ministry called *Renewed*, an offshoot of his prison ministry. It was a 501(c)(3) ministry, a post-release halfway house, much like the Denton House, but not as well funded. All who served there did so with compassion. For a while, Marshall had no one in the house to hold the guys accountable, so the discipline of the men suffered until a volunteer stepped up. Once Marshall finally got more help, the ministry thrived throughout the time Marshall led it.

Things at home were so stable and happy that Marshall sometimes wondered when the bottom might fall out. Kali was twelve and Imani was eight, and Katika worked part-time as an independent model. Her clients included Macy's and Higbee's and other area department stores. By 1986, Keith graduated from high school and enlisted in the Navy. Even though Keith was of age and joined the military, Marshall and Tik fully encouraged him as the son he had become.

As new believers, Marshall and Katika had been unaware of Christian schools. By the time they heard of them, Keith had already graduated, or they would have sent him to one. They sent Kali and Imani to Christian schools, starting with pre-K. Each step required an application and approval, but Marshall and Katika wanted their children to be taught in schools that honored the Lord Jesus.

Both went through Chapel Hill Christian School, and in seventh grade, Kali went to Cuyahoga Valley Christian Academy (CVCA). At Chapel Hill, Kali started playing basketball, and he continued playing at CVCA while Imani remained at Chapel Hill.

Rumors persisted for five years that the power plant where Marshall worked was to be closed. In 1992 the rumors came to fruition, and Marshall moved to a different position within the company as an equipment operator, running trenchers and Bobcats. At the Gorge Power Plant, he took part in the production of electricity. He helped transmit and distribute electricity and, after training, became proficient at his new job assignment. He still relished his job at the company and hoped to retire after a long and fruitful career.

He remained peaceful with full-time work and ministries, and he began to feel this was the path God had for him.

Okay, I'll continue on with the jail ministry and work on until God changes my course.

But more roadblocks were coming.

———

Marshall's new position mandated he work in different areas covered by Ohio Edison. One of the first places he was assigned was a bedroom community south of Cleveland. The area, over ninety-seven percent White, had not fully integrated, even as late as 1992. Hence the city experienced more racial hangover for a longer period as if in a time warp, the Civil Rights movement a foreign concept.

Working in this area segregated by geography and choice, Marshall felt uncomfortable at best. As one of the few Black guys working in the neighborhood, Marshall ran into some White Edison employees he sensed itched for trouble. *Oh man, these guys look like racist rednecks. What's next?*

He didn't have to wait long to find out.

"Brandon, did you bring your gun with you?" one of them said. "I brought mine."

"Yeah, I got it, uh-huh," Marshall said, even though he didn't. He retained working knowledge of his past street language of intimidation and fear, and he still carried some racial anger. "Just know I am a Christian, and I am carrying."

The guy challenged Marshall, yet the Spirit challenged Marshall to stand his ground, but with grace.

Lord, how do I handle this in a way that will bring You honor and save my butt?

The young challenger, Marshall figured, tried to make a name for himself in front of his peers. The other workers didn't know about Marshall's history, which could have stopped the taunter's tirade. Not knowing with whom he dealt, the younger man screamed insults at Marshall and tried to embarrass him.

Marshall leaned into him. "You don't have to talk to me like that. I'm here to work together. Don't yell at me anymore. Yelling at me crosses the line."

He turned to walk away, but the young man continued to shout obscenities at him. "You son of a b—! Go home and tell your old lady you might be able to learn this job, if I let you!" Marshall stopped but did not turn to face his taunter yet. He felt his fists ball up as his rage awakened. The young man continued to yell and laugh as Marshall fought the demons that should have remained in his past.

Lord, I'm desperate for Your help.

He fought the strong urge to turn around and deck the guy.

Marshall put his dog on, turned to face the harasser, and said, "Work with me, here. I'm not just off the street; I've got history. Don't mess with me."

The guy didn't let up. The workers around them stopped to watch.

Marshall said, "Just tell me what you need, and I'll get it."

He knew the man had chosen Marshall as his personal object of wrath. The foreman said nothing, and the leaders on the other crew said nothing either. That angered Marshall. This young man was trying to build his reputation as a tough guy using Marshall as his step stool.

"Man, you don't know nothin'. You're just a stupid Black son of a—."

Marshall, dog fully on, eased toward the guy and did not take his eyes off him. He stared at him with a look of hate and merited retribution. The other guys moved in closer, and Marshall worried they'd all jump him.

As Marshall walked toward him, the guy looked at Marshall's face and clenched fists, and backed away. The other guys followed suit when the wanna-be bully said, "Okay, man, I'm sorry."

Marshall stepped toward him and stood eyeball-to-eyeball with his harasser.

"Let me tell you something," Marshall said. The guy looked down at the largest fists Marshall hoped he'd ever seen. "You ever talk to me like that again, I'll break your neck. Do you understand me?" For full effect, he asked him again, "Do you understand me?"

"Yeah, man. Sorry, man."

Marshall faced the crew who gathered to watch the now-deflated confrontation.

"Anybody got a problem with that?"

In unison, they said, "No. No, Marshall."

Marshall got back into the service truck and confronted the foreman, who watched the whole scenario unfold and did nothing. "Listen. *You* let this stuff go on. Nobody talks to me like that—do you understand me?"

"Yes, Marshall, I sure do," the foreman said.

Lord, thank You for showing me Your power, for keeping my fists from pummeling that racist punk.

He chuckled to himself as he considered other choice names for the guy.

And, Lord, forgive me, please, for the names I am calling him.

Marshall never had another problem with the guys in that community; he got their respect by standing his ground without raising his voice or his fists, much as he wanted to. He wasn't purely happy with the way he handled the situation, but he gained a lot of credit with them, and that opened doors for him to share his faith and the Gospel. As time passed, Marshall turned into a mediator within the crews. He was leading, not following the ways of the world, and he turned into a soothing presence.

Within the space of a year, the energy company switched Marshall's job. They relegated him to a meter reader, albeit with no pay cut. As much as he wanted to retire from the previous two jobs he held within the company, he wished to be delivered from meter-reading.

He detested it. After sixteen years with the company, he felt like this move shoved him back to square one, and he suspected discrimination. This job was difficult and sometimes dangerous, but he needed to work and support his family. So, he continued to consider it a mission field and bloomed where God planted him.

Marshall persisted as a good employee—he always showed up ready to work. In this new position, he also spoke for the union as their safety director. God let him use and hone his speaking skills in this respect, and he enjoyed the opportunities.

Yet meter-reading was isolated, each reader having a solo route. The only people he interacted with were those at the shop where he reported in and reported back after a day in the field. Each day he went somewhere different—Akron, Medina, Brunswick, and many other nearby communities, including Hudson.

His daily process began as he received his route for the day; a reader must get so many meters read during their appointed daily hours. He knew he couldn't goof off, nor did he want to. He was already in good shape; the job even improved his physical condition because he had to walk a lot. Working was also like training for him and helped him prepare for the marathons he was running at the time. Through the YMCA where he exercised, he ran a few in Akron and recently connected with the annual Marine's marathon in Washington, DC. In his head, he thought, *These guys are actually paying me to work out! Cool.*

Angry dogs provided the only danger to Marshall. He scaled the fence of one house to read the meter. As he went over, he looked around the yard and into the eyes of two German shepherds. He froze. The dogs didn't.

Oh, Lord!

Boom! He turned around and split for the fence. As he jumped the fence, the dogs ran headlong into it. He ran into the street, adrenaline pumping, breathing hard, and laughing all the way.

God! This is crazy! Why am I out here? All I am doing is trying to serve You, Lord, and here I am. I hate this job. I'm out here all by myself. Me and these dogs!

He got better at sniffing out where dogs lived and thankfully never got bit while on that job. But as he talked with God, which he had a lot of time to do while reading meters, he began to realize God was in the process of removing his dependence on any job and placing more of his dependence on Him.

God said to Marshall, "It's Me. I've got you."

No one in management ever gave Marshall a performance review. He received no attaboys or words of affirmation about doing a good job. The only indicator that he was appreciated was when he received a heavier load of meters to read. A worker could leave for the day once his reading was complete, and he fell into the trap of slowing down a bit and taking a long lunch, so they wouldn't "reward" him with a harder route the next day.

It was a trial that could have led to complacency.

CHAPTER SEVENTEEN

A HAVEN

Marshall talked a lot to God while he worked his routes. He trudged through snow and slipped on the ice and asked God again and again, *Why am I out here, Lord?*

No matter the conditions, meters had to be read; snow, ice, mud—nothing kept him from his appointed route, and he felt mailmen had nothing on meter readers. God allowed difficult times within a detested job, and Marshall learned to be faithful. As he walked and prayed and learned to be patient with God, a wonderful job opportunity came up.

One of the pastors at the church he attended sought Marshall after a service. "Marshall, I hear the Haven of Rest is hiring."

"The Haven?" Marshall said. "That's a homeless mission. I'm not interested in any Haven of Rest."

"Brother," the pastor said, "why don't you just go see what they are talking about; go apply."

And Marshall thought, *Okay, how can it hurt to just go interview?*

The Haven of Rest sits near the middle of Akron, close to where Marshall and Katika lived. It was founded in 1943 by a Christian couple who held a special love for homeless, destitute people. The Haven provides meals for people on the streets and rooms where homeless men and women can sleep in safety. Their programs and offerings include job training, outreach, clothing, and food distribution, meals on the premises, and spiritual encouragement and growth. Marshall called the Haven and scheduled an interview with the director. During the appointment, Marshall thought, *I know nothing about homeless people.* Yet as he took a tour of the facility, he saw the ministry in action. He recognized how God obviously worked there. He also noticed many men he knew during his prison ministry visits to area jails.

Throughout the tour, he heard, "Hey, Reverend Brandon, remember me from Summit County Jail, and other jails." He also heard from men he met at other area jails.

Impressed by what the Haven did for these men, Marshall knew God made that connection for him. He believed he could be an agent for change in the lives of homeless and hopeless men. He saw the vision of these broken men changed by God's power, just as he had been. He had the strong sense God wanted him there.

During that first visit, he told the director, "Whoa, man, I had no clue. This is so amazing."

He returned home and shared his interview impressions with his wife, and they prayed about Marshall's possible job change. With a second interview scheduled, Tik asked Marshall about the salary. "Well, what kind of money are they talking about?"

Marshall said, "I don't know. I'll ask them."

He made a decent salary at Ohio Edison, and it allowed them to keep sending their children to Christian schools. Money did not mean everything to the Brandons, but it was important Marshall *not* take a salary cut. They knew this opportunity also involved a lesson from the Lord: Would they trust Him for the outcome or not?

At the second interview, he asked about the salary.

The interviewer said, "It's our policy not to discuss money until we make a job offer."

Marshall still felt a strong call to work there and minister to these men. He felt the ministry team and the residents liked him, and he certainly liked the people with whom he might be working. The director and his wife took Marshall and Katika out to dinner to meet her and gauge their marital relationship and how the job might impact it.

They asked her, "Are you willing to come on board as the spouse of an employee?" and "Are you comfortable with your husband working with such a ministry as ours?"

"Yes, I am," Katika answered to both questions. Then she asked, "What kind of salary are we talking here?"

They reiterated their policy not to talk money until they made a job offer.

Marshall and Katika prayed together about the job and prayed separately about the least amount of money they could accept to care for their family. After they prayed separately, they came back together, and each shared the amount that God had revealed to them—the same amount, the exact same amount.

"All right," said Marshall, "that's kind of a sign that God is in this."

Katika agreed. "I don't doubt He is."

When the final interview came, the Haven made a formal job offer to Marshall. "Marshall, we like you and want you to come work with us."

Okay, I can finally ask them how much the salary will be.

Marshall fully expected the amount to be what he and Tik had prayed about. "Great, please tell me the salary."

When they told him, Marshall cried. It was so far below the minimum he and Tik knew they needed he was overcome. He tried to pawn off his tears as laughter and said, "Is that negotiable?" He wiped tears as he tried to laugh.

"No, the board sets the policy each year, and it will not be changed until next year." "Let me go home and discuss this with my wife," Marshall said, "and I'll get back to you."

When he got home, he told Katika what they offered.

"You didn't take it, did you?" Katika was nearly in tears herself.

"No, Baby, I didn't take it." And he chuckled, this time without crying.

Tik continued, "Because the only way we can afford that is if they give us room and board and set up a little 'Brandon family wing' in the corner."

They both let out a sigh of relief and got a good laugh out of it. There was no way, they decided, they could live on the amount the Haven offered.

Marshall called them the next day and said, "Thanks for the offer, but we can't afford to take it. It's not enough money for us because we have two children in Christian schools. I'm in my forties, not a young man just out of college. I really need to make a larger salary."

Marshall felt he was living by this ironic adage: "Lord, You keep me humble, and the world will keep me broke."

The next Sunday at church, the pastor who had referred him to the Haven said, "Marshall, I want to see you after service."

When Marshall stopped by his office, the pastor said, "I hear you are interested in this job at the Haven. We would like to give you some money toward it." The pastor handed Marshall a note and said, "Here is what we can give you per year toward your job."

Marshall looked at the number and stood as though stuck to the floor; the amount the church promised him plus the offered salary was within $500 of what he and Katika had prayed about.

Oh, Lord, You are amazing!

Marshall wanted to whoop and holler; it took all the decorum he could muster to simply say, "Thank you. I hope the job is still available. I'll call them tomorrow."

Marshall and Katika had their own worship service at home that night, praising the Lord.

Marshall called the Haven the next day.

"Marshall," the director said, "we had two candidates we wanted to offer the job. We've been trying to call the other guy and cannot reach him. But we really want you for the job." *Lord, I repeat what I said earlier. You are amazing!*

Marshall told them he would accept the job and shared the good news with his wife. "Lord," Marshall said, "we are so humbled by how You lead us. We ask you to take this job and make it Yours. Work though me and bring glory to Your name."

Katika added, "Father, we love You. We give this all to you in humble thanksgiving. Lead us and guide us in this ministry, and let Your name be praised."

"And Lord," Marshall prayed, "help me make a smooth transition from Ohio Edison to this new job. Let me be a light to them even as I leave the job. Instead of them telling me not to let the door hit me where the good Lord split me, let them give me a holy kiss goodbye." When he went into work the next day and gave his two-week notice, news filtered through the ranks.

"What are you, crazy, Brandon?" the guys said. "You've been here seventeen years and you're going to leave to go to a ministry?"

Marshall smiled to himself and thought, *This is how I choose to follow the Lord—how I choose to trust Him for everything.*

Marshall started at the Haven of Rest in July 1995, and he hoped this vocation would be the one he could retire from.

At that time, Kali (fifteen) and Imani (eleven) were fully engaged at their church and had been baptized there, choosing to follow Jesus as Lord. Marshall laughed at his daughter a lot. One time when she was three or four, he corrected her about something, and she looked at him and said, "Daddy, you're 'busin' (abusing) me." As he laughed, he wondered how she even knew what abuse was.

I thank God she doesn't know what it truly is. May this verbal admonition be the worst she ever endures.

Everything did not run smoothly for the Brandons after Marshall made the switch to the Haven. He knew they faced spiritual attack, which is when the evil one tries to mess with the people of God. They just scraped by as they trusted God with every day.

Then came the problems at their house. Their furnace quit one winter, the roof went bad, and they went for a while with only one borrowed car. Both had jobs, so Marshall took the bus and Tik used the running car to get to her place of work. Despite the hardships, Marshall saw the whole situation as an opportunity to trust God. He knew God was faithful to provide all they needed, and they never missed a beat.

God sent somebody to help with each problem as it arose. Through the church, people heard there was a need and stepped up to help, both financially and with tradespeople who fixed many of the issues the Brandons had with their house.

But as the tests of their faith continued, God provided.

Kali switched from basketball to football while in high school at CVCA, and Marshall and Tik attended games and became friends with other team members' parents, including Joe and Karen Coffey, whose son Jeremy was a good friend of Kali's. The families often rode together to out-of-town games, and Joe and Marshall shared their histories with each other. Joe served as an associate pastor at Hudson Community Chapel (HCC) and knew of the financial hardships Marshall was facing.

One day Joe said, "Marshall, our ministry makes a lot more money than you, and we want to help you."

Not once had Marshall asked for help; Joe just offered. Through the benevolence fund at Hudson Community Chapel, Marshall and Katika's roof was repaired.

One of the greatest demonstrations of God's grace Marshall ever saw happened through Joe. He called Marshall and said, "Why don't we get together for lunch this week?" Marshall thought Joe would come to the Haven and meet at the office, and he did. But then Joe said, "Let's take a ride."

They got in Joe's car and drove to the office of a man Joe discipled. Joe told Marshall about him on the way, and Marshall learned of his wealth. "I want you to meet him and tell him your testimony," Joe said.

After Marshall shared an abbreviated but emotionally packed testimony with him, the man asked, "What kind of car are you driving?"

"A borrowed car from a friend at church," Marshall said.

"I want to buy you a car," the man said.

"Huh?"

Marshall couldn't move, amazed and struck dumb by God's grace.

Father God, I'm going to have to start wearing boots.

Marshall hadn't told the man that his family needed two cars, but he realized Joe had given this man a heads-up about his need.

"There's a dealer across the street," he said. "Let's go over."

When they arrived, the dealer brought an exceptionally clean, used car around to the front of the lot.

"Do you like this car?" the wealthy man asked Marshall.

"Well, yeah," Marshall said.

Anything with four tires and a running engine was a vast improvement.

"Okay, I'm going to buy it for you," the man said.

"What?"

The benefactor smiled and put his hand on Marshall's shoulder. "Marshall, I want to buy you a car. The Lord blessed me with enough to help others. I want the blessing of helping you. Will you allow me?"

"What can I do for you for this?" Marshall didn't receive it well and felt the need to compensate in some way. "Can I come wash your car every day? Can I come cut your grass?" "No, man, you can do nothing but receive this," the man said as he went inside to write the check for the car. Taxes, title—all was taken care of; all Marshall had to do was get in and drive it. That's all he *could* do.

As Marshall reflected on that amazing act of grace, he thought about what he learned in God's Word about living the life of a Christian: It's easy to give, but receiving is hard. That's why Scripture says it's better to give than receive. Receiving means a person is in a position of need. Giving means a person can bless. Yet both are a blessing. The receiving part is hard because it works on one's pride. Grace is a free gift of God; a man can do nothing to earn or deserve it.

Joe Coffey served at HCC with Jim Colledge, the founding pastor. Both men were White, as was most of the congregation. Jim's wife, Barb, worked with Katika at an abstinence ministry in Akron, and Marshall and Jim previously met at their wives' ministry's Christmas party. As their wives mingled with friends at that year's party, Jim and Marshall got to know each other's histories. They ended up talking about race relations. Marshall could hardly believe he was having this conversation with a White man.

Wow, Lord. What is going to come of this?

Marshall learned how to look for the ways God worked in all the situations of his life.

After they'd talked a while that night, Jim said, "Hey, you want to get together maybe sometime for lunch, and we can continue this conversation?"

"I'd love to."

Marshall really liked Jim, and he met with him a few times before the meeting when Joe introduced Marshall to the man who bought the car for him.

At first, he didn't know Jim and Joe served together, but he soon caught on to the connection once he and Jim started meeting regularly at a local restaurant. Their conversations centered on their life stories, race relations, and diversity in the church.

Throughout these weeks and months, Marshall was in the midst of an exceptional period of growth at the Haven of Rest and in a good place in his life spiritually. His job at the Haven fit him well. He understood the guys who came in, their addictions, and their survivor lifestyles. He became manager of the Haven's residential program, which involved long-term drug rehab. He stepped right in like he'd been doing it all his life. He loved on those guys and expanded his ever-growing heart as he shared God's love with them.

A wonderful thing happened as he ministered to them; he also became an unofficial minister and counselor to the staff. The love he showed them overflowed with the love he had for the men with whom he worked and encouraged.

Ah, now this is the place I get to retire from.

Yet Marshall somehow knew through all of it that God was preparing him for something else. *What are You going to do next, Lord?*

During a lunchtime conversation, Joe delivered a bombshell to Marshall. "You know, we've been talking," he told Marshall. "We're going to hire a guy for evangelism and discipleship. Guess whose name came up?"

Marshall stammered, "Uh . . . whose?"

Joe smiled. "Yours."

Lord? I'm to go to Hudson—lily-white, affluent Hudson? Me? Marshall Brandon? He looked at Joe and said, "Come on. I can't do that."

"Just pray about it, Marshall. We're not going to do this for another year anyhow." Marshall got into his new-to-him car and drove home, thankful he didn't have to think while driving because he was awestruck by how God moved in his life. *Wow, God. You are so awesome!*

He walked into the house and said to Tik, "Come outside. I want to show you something."

Tik followed him out, saw the car, and wept. No words could describe how they both felt. Marshall thought about how they scraped by, going on faith. No professionals came to their rescue before. It was always, "Call backyard Billy to come see what he can do to get this borrowed car running." Their whole way of life had been survival mode. His faith got stretched in inconceivable ways, and he could sense God saying, "Hey, I've got you."

This God does *provide*, Marshall thought as he dropped to his knees in their driveway with Katika at his side.

God reminded Marshall, "Just rest in Me. I got you."

Marshall had seen many turning points in his solo life, and now he saw greater turning points in his life as partner to Katika, father, friend, employee, and church leader. His trust in God bloomed as he placed more and more faith in Him because he learned provision comes from Him. God uses whomever and whatever He wants to provide for us, His people, both spiritually and in our physical needs.

For the next year, Marshall and Katika prayed, as Marshall assumed Jim and Joe and the church elders did, about the possible move to the Hudson church.

Marshall and Katika had been at their church in Akron for twenty-three years, so the prospect of leaving people who had become their family daunted them. Both had become leaders within the congregation, and Marshall had preached a number of times. He still had his jail and prison ministry and taught an adult Bible fellowship class. In addition, Marshall led the arts theater, helping with the inception and production of plays. But during that year of prayer, as they grew in the grace and knowledge of the Lord Jesus, so too did their discernment. In time, Marshall and Katika decided a change was in the offing.

A group of people from their current church who agreed with their call for a change came to the couple and said, "We are thinking of leaving and starting a new church. Will you be our pastor?"

Since nothing was solidified with Hudson Community Chapel yet, and Marshall and Katika indeed felt called to leave the church, they said they would pray about it.

After he and Katika took three weeks to pray, they agreed Marshall would lead that band of believers in the new venture of a church plant. The small group met, prayed, and formed organizational committees.

When he told Joe what was going on and the group looked for a building, Marshall noticed a deep change in Joe's countenance. He looked at his face and thought, *What's up with this face? Did I just do something wrong? He sure doesn't look happy for us.*

Joe remained still for a moment and said, "Marshall, before you go any further with your group, will you hear me out?"

"Why, yes, of course."

"We'd like to be a church with more diversity. We'd like you to consider coming to Hudson and bringing your people with you."

Marshall said, "Hudson?" The thought of asking and then leading his group of African Americans to an all-White church left a sour taste in his mouth.

CHAPTER EIGHTEEN

HUDSON?

Marshall thought about Joe's offer, but he thought more about his response.

Hmmm, I guess I'm still carrying some anger. Lord, I need Your great help, again.

He again voiced aloud, "Hudson?"

Joe said, "Yeah, Hudson. We'd like you to be our pastor of discipleship and evangelism. Even if your group says no, we still want you to come."

For the second time, Marshall stood in wet cement, feeling like the rest of him was going to sink.

Lord? What am I supposed to do? This is an incredible privilege to be faced with such a choice. What about my past, my past that includes such hate for the White man who would keep me down, kicked to the curb? And here You are sending two White men I now love asking me to walk into an all-White setting, to hopefully affect change that will bring Black and White people together in praise of You. I am overwhelmed, Lord. How can I say no?

Marshall told Joe he would speak to his wife and the group, and then they would all pray about it. When he got home that day, he and Tik sat in their living room while supper cooked.

"I met with Joe Coffey today," Marshall said.

"Really?" Tik said, "Is something up with Jeremy and football?"

"Um, no. He asked me to come to Hudson Community Chapel as the new pastor of evangelism and discipleship."

He waited for her reaction, not without a bit of trepidation.

"Hudson?"

"Yes, Hudson." He felt like he was watching a replay of his conversation with Joe.

"Hudson?" she repeated.

"Ditto. I had the same reaction."

"Well, honey, what do you think?"

Marshall told her how he thought the Lord led him on this move, and God's conviction made a strong case for affecting change.

"But they won't make us be like them, will they? I mean, we can still be ourselves, right?"

Marshall knew what she was saying. Would they lose their cultural identity and be swallowed up in a sea of Whiteness?

"Let's pray about it and ask our people to pray too," Katika said. "You know you have my support."

She walked to the kitchen and shook her head. "Hudson?"

Marshall had to regroup before he went back to his people to propose the idea of joining the all-White church. He stood astounded at the possibilities facing him and the people who called him their pastor. At their next meeting, he broached the subject as presented by Joe.

To a person, they said, "Hudson?"

Marshall had to chuckle. He said, "Please pray about it, and don't make a decision now. See what the Lord says, and we will meet again next week."

The following week, the group gathered. Marshall was barraged with questions and concerns.

"Will they receive us?"

"What will it be like for me to hold a White baby in the nursery?"

"Will they trust me?"

"Will my children be accepted?"

Marshall couldn't answer all their questions, so he proposed another meeting. "Let's ask Jim and Joe to come down and meet with us, so you can ask them your questions directly."

The group agreed, and Marshall set up the meeting. The men from lily-white Hudson came to meet with the courteous but cautious group of African Americans. Joe and Jim answered their questions head-on and assured the people that, indeed, they would be welcomed. Their warmth and sincerity seemed genuine to Marshall and all his church members.

After Jim and Joe left, Marshall said, "Well, what do you think?"

"Okay, we'll give it a try. We will do it—let's do it," the people said as their reticence turned to cautious excitement.

"Okay," Marshall said, "I am going to pray some more about it. But having your support means a lot to me."

All that remained was for Marshall to give Jim and Joe his answer. Marshall and Katika were still overwhelmed by the situation.

He wondered, *What does it mean to be a full-time pastor in an almost all-White church?*

Gifted as a pastor-shepherd, he used that gift at the homeless mission. He knew his time at the Haven prepared him for what came next, and Hudson probably fit the bill. But he still felt overwhelmed. Ordained but never with the official title of pastor, he knew the position at Hudson came in God's timing, not his.

In his anxiety, he prayed, *Lord, I don't know how to do this. Who am I? I'm just a sinner, a street kid from Youngstown. Help me, Lord, to do this well and to bring You glory.*

His sleep was interrupted as he wrestled with God. The Spirit within him woke him in the middle of many nights and called him to go and do what the Lord placed in his path.

Lord, I can't do this.

And Marshall's faithful God supernaturally said, "You're right. *You* cannot do this. But *I* can do it through you. I want you to go."

With confidence brought by his trust in God and the support of his beloved wife, Marshall contacted Jim and Joe and told them he accepted the position and his group would join him and Katika in Hudson.

That confidence tempered his lingering doubts, not in God, but in his ability to enter and fit into the Hudson milieu of affluence, advanced education, and—yes—Whiteness. A little distrust of White man's authority and disregard for a Black man's struggle still held a grip on his heart. His courage tried to outweigh the doubts, but they lingered. He had to step out in faith, knowing he had to trust God in all of it. Indeed, some children who attended the Hudson church with their parents never saw a Black family up close, even at the beginning of a new millennium. Marshall had a burden to be one of God's agents of change.

At the time, Hudson Community Chapel (HCC) recently completed a new building project. When the doors opened in June 2000, a small band of African Americans entered as well. The Lord prepared the way for all of them to enter the new church building together, as one people united in Christ.

For Marshall, that situation made the transition easier. Everyone who entered the new building went in "new," even those who had been members of the congregation for years. Marshall felt a spark of excitement at what God would do in and through each of them. At the first service, Marshall and his group were introduced to the congregation, and leadership scheduled a panel discussion to answer questions from the congregation. Its title? "Everything You Wanted to Know About Black People but Were Afraid to Ask."

On the evening of the Q and A panel, hands shot up like flares. That's the only way Marshall could describe the differences that his group's presence brought to HCC. Within six months of their arrival, a number of these church-family sessions were held with a panel of both Black and

White members of the church. Pastors Jim, Joe, and Marshall formed an integral part of the panel, and a few elders and others from Marshall's group added to the mix. To make the transition smooth, communication had to be up-front and timely.

Hundreds of people attended the sessions, and before the first panel, Marshall questioned the congregation's needs. He sensed his people were nervous, just as he and Katika. One of the first questions was, "Why?"

Marshall took that one, "Because God tells us we are one in Him."

He quoted Ephesians 4:1–6, which says, "I, therefore, a prisoner for the Lord, urge you to walk in a manner worthy of the calling to which you have been called, with all humility and gentleness, with patience, bearing with one another in love, eager to maintain the unity of the Spirit in the bond of peace. There is one body and one Spirit—just as you were called to the one hope that belongs to your call— one Lord, one faith, one baptism, one God and Father of all, who is over all and through all and in all."

He continued, "We are all made in the image of God, and whether we are light-skinned or dark-skinned, we belong to Him. It's good to come together to worship the Lord. My intent is to love you as Christ loves us."

Most of the other questions had to do with the differences in worship styles and what each group could do to make things more comfortable for everyone. The discussion created a strong start to open the channels of diversity. Marshall planned events that brought people of all colors together, and slowly the invisible trench of separation was filled with the Gospel and the Spirit of God.

One of the things that hurt Marshall's heart was his children's acceptance of the move, or rather their lack of acceptance. Imani chose to attend a pre-dominantly African American church in Akron. Kali, who came to Hudson for only a short while, chose instead to attend a Baptist church in West Akron. They supported their parents, but not by making the leap to Hudson.

Marshall remained undeterred and wanted the congregation to be comfortable with him. He wandered the halls on Sunday mornings and introduced himself. He went to the nursery area and met the little ones. One four-year-old girl smiled as she looked up at him, shaking his massive hands with her teeny fingers. She said, "Pastor Bwandon, you're bwown." Marshall laughed with his loud, warm voice and swore he'd never forget that.

I can go a long way on that. The honesty and sweetness of a child is what we all need. Marshall's new title was what Jim and Joe promised to him: pastor of evangelism and discipleship. He directed efforts to help grow the congregation in their role as believers who boldly share their faith. His responsibilities also included building a bridge between the suburb of Hudson and inner-city Akron. He served as the connector between the church in Hudson and those in need. Marshall, both through his years in prison ministry and at the Haven of Rest, knew a large network of para-church organizations with which HCC could minister to the oppressed and needy.

Parachurch organizations are Christian entities that provide ministries such as employment assistance, after-school care, Bible teaching, and training outside the church environment. They meet people where they are and usually set up their organizations within the neighborhoods where needs are most concentrated. Parachurch organizations then refer people to various churches for meeting needs and connecting people to resources.

Marshall started a prison ministry at HCC right away and soon gained a large group of volunteers who served alongside him as he led worship services in the jails. He also taught an Adult Bible Fellowship (ABF) class for people new to Christianity called Firm Foundations. Through this ABF, Marshall and Katika made numerous friendships he knew would endure for the rest of his life.

Marshall initiated many outreaches where the affluent and educated people of Hudson could lend their financial and administrative talents. Thanksgiving and Christmas outreaches annually reached thousands of people in the inner city. He watched God raise up many ministries to meet diverse needs.

Benevolence was one of Marshall's other duties at HCC. Throughout each week, people who sought help, usually financial, from HCC came to the office. Marshall used his street-smart discernment to sense genuine need from those who were not truly deprived. Many times, he sent someone away with nothing and later found out the person went from church to church with the same lie.

Amid the joy of what Marshall saw happening within the congregation, a major hurdle for him to overcome was the temporal thinking of others. Some pastors (the church had at least five different pastors) and leaders within HCC posed the question: "What's in this for us?

How are these parachurch ministries going to affect our financial and congregational growth?

What's our payback?"

Financial payback? Where is God in this? Oh, Lord, what have You gotten me into?

CHAPTER NINETEEN

OWNING THE ROLE

Marshall's answer to questions he faced about "value" to the church of the ministries he led was always, "How much is a soul worth?"

Leaders were baffled by his approach, his thinking. One day one of them confronted Marshall. "You're Kingdom-minded, aren't you?"

"Why, yes, absolutely! It's all about the Kingdom. It's not just about a single congregation; it's about God's Kingdom here on earth," Marshall said. "Every person we reach will affect the Kingdom. They may not end up attending HCC or increasing our pot, but they are an important part of what God is doing here."

"You really believe that they will not drain us?"

"I do believe that. These people are being redeemed, restored, renewed! It's about God!"

Once they understood him, he gained respect from within the pastoral staff as well as the congregation. Marshall watched Jim and Joe continually back him up, and he grew more comfortable, not feeling rejected or unwanted. He used his street survival techniques to read people. Not once did he sense someone at HCC was condescending to him. He began to grow more spiritually and once again found himself in the role of shepherd to staff members.

Marshall took that role seriously and relished the metaphor of a pastor as a shepherd. His philosophy was that a shepherd ought to smell like his sheep. People need to be able to engage with and "touch" their shepherd. He was among the sheep—he smelled like them, herded his flock, picked them up, felt their pain, and struggled with them. He encouraged them and rebuked them. He got his shepherd's staff out and give them a spiritual lickin' every now and then to set them back on the right course.

Marshall's sheep knew him and understood he gave rebukes with love and compassion. Marshall believed God loves all people, including the broken, and he displayed the love and grace God showed him. He considered his role as a pastor to be multifaceted, with all his different talents, experiences, and gifts brought together as a whole package.

One unfortunate pushback Marshall encountered had to do with his office. As with many church operations, the building's color scheme came through a committee, and it was "institutional beige," which reminded Marshall of prison. Katika is adept at interior design, and she and Marshall decided to paint his office to reflect his heritage and love of color. Katika brought in her paint chips and painted small sample spots on Marshall's walls. By the time the painters were in the room and had started to paint the walls, they were told to stop. Katika was angry; so was Marshall. It became more than just a conformity issue regarding the decorating scheme of the building. In Marshall's eyes, it morphed into an issue about freedom.

A week went by without a resolution, and Marshall, usually gregarious, shut down. He didn't grumble to anyone but his wife and assistant, but he did not back down about modifying his space to suit his needs.

"Yo, Marshall," his assistant said. "You going to go Youngstown on them?" referring to his dark days in the gangs.

They laughed together, but both understood the serious nature of the issue.

Marshall remained steadfast and assertively made his case, and his office was painted to his liking within a week. Everyone who visited him said what a lively, comfortable space it was, even those who initially protested the change.

We won 'em over, Lord. Thank You.

In the first few years at HCC, Marshall preached a few times. He taught at his former church and had preached infrequently, but preaching to White folks? In a Black congregation, Marshall knew his audience and which illustrations would resonate with them. Even when he spoke at the Haven of Rest, the people he ministered to came from the same background as his.

At Hudson, he spoke to an affluent audience with whom he had little in common but their mutual faith. He tried to be himself, but he struggled because of cultural differences. Not that Marshall didn't love to share the Word; it overjoyed him to proclaim the Gospel and see people respond in surrender to the Lord who would free their souls. No, the burden he felt was the more buttoned-up style of White people's worship.

It's no wonder they are called "the Frozen Chosen," Marshall chuckled to himself more than a few times.

A hindrance, yes, but not insurmountable. The Lord gifted Marshall with a joy that could not be squelched (for long) by any circumstances.

He loved these people from the depths of his heart, but they had no visible response to his teaching of the Word that he could see. At HCC, the people responded individually, privately, quietly. They paid sharp attention, yet their verbal response was usually subdued. To Marshall, the White congregation looked at a sermon as a time of teaching, not celebration. Marshall received encouraging comments after he spoke, knowing the sermons the Lord had directed him to give were heard and, he prayed, acted on. But he yearned for the immediate call and response he knew in Black houses of worship.

In Black churches, people often respond corporately, with spontaneous gestures of praise that emanate from the congregation. Each worship service is a celebration of what God has done. When the preacher speaks truth that touches the hearts of the people, many hearty amens are heard. It's not uncommon for Black folks to shout, "Preach it, brother!" Clapping erupts when words fail, and, all in all, it's a joyful, loud service.

The music presented another difference, a big one. While the musicians at HCC were excellent, even professional, Marshall felt they needed more diversity of worship music selections. Part of his reason for accepting the position there was to help increase the diversity at HCC, so, working with the music ministry, he helped introduce some Gospel music authored by Black Christian artists.

As a preamble, whenever he spoke to the congregation, Marshall said, "Okay, you are allowed to say amen while I preach. You can clap or shout words of affirmation. Can I get an amen?"

The people responded, to Marshall's great delight, happy the congregation could accept what he had to say and react in such a kind manner. Some people continued to respond throughout his messages with no cues from him.

Marshall also felt altar calls were important to give people a chance to come forward and say yes to the Lord God's kind invitation and become Christians. He made calls to the altar a regular part of his messages whenever he taught from the pulpit.

Black History Month also became a new and special annual event at HCC. Marshall planned the inaugural night, "Celebration of Martin Luther King Jr." People filled the sanctuary, which held close to a thousand souls. Marshall bubbled with excitement as he told his story and spoke of the great progress made in America regarding race relations. He thanked the HCC congregation for their willingness to embrace diversity and shared his hope that it would spark a wildfire of great race relations within the church. It was a blessed night for him; he felt he had made great strides in showing the congregation how privileged he felt to be part of the unity God was orchestrating within the church.

If only everyone had been on board.

———

"Lisa, can you come into my office?" Marshall said to his assistant.

As she sat in front of him, he shared part of his heart with her.

Marshall understood that for people to grow together, they must share their histories and heal. What happened in America in the eighteenth and nineteenth centuries is still a national scar; slavery created a chasm between Whites and Blacks. As God's people, Marshall knew complete healing can only be based on becoming like Christ, not in preserving the chasm.

He asked Lisa to pray about helping him start a group to help heal the rift. Common Ground began, led by one of the Black members who had come to Hudson with the Brandons. Common Ground was created to facilitate four principal goals: (1) the acknowledgment that God created the races to bring glory to Him, no matter what their color; (2) healing needed to take place; (3) people would be brought together through diverse events and informational meetings, and (4) all would strive to grow to be more like Jesus. As an offshoot of Common Ground, a group called Bridge Builders was formed, a social interaction tool for diversity, pairing groups to have dinners and enjoy social occasions together.

Both groups served to join people of different skin color, and, as a result, many deep, lasting friendships developed. Marshall and Katika thanked God for the growth they witnessed. Yet, some people chose not to let the past go. They forged a sword that kept the injustice of slavery alive in their hearts and minds. Unbiblical and divisive, it eventually led to the demise of Common Ground.

One of the things the Lord removed from Marshall was his predisposition for angry confrontation. Even today, Marshall gets frustrated but is quick to temper it with a self-admonition of his bitter roots. At the time, his assistant marveled aloud about his ability to let things go. Marshall still became frustrated and angry, however, with people who try to foist their deep-seated racial attitudes onto all White men. He believed this worked against a spirit of reconciliation and bred mistrust. Marshall kept his cool, was quick to forgive, and displayed wisdom as well. At that point, he felt it was better to trust relationships would grow from what they had already seeded.

Marshall continued to be grateful for how God worked in his life. He didn't take any of what happened for granted regarding the opportunities God had given him to represent the Lord to this community. This understanding so impacted him that he changed his sign-off in emails, texts, and letters to "Ambassador for Christ." Ministry flourished in his office, including prayer with many people to receive Jesus Christ as their Savior.

As a result of his personal ministry to so many, Ina, one of the members of the ABF that he led, came to see him one day.

"Pastor Brandon," she said, "I wonder if you would come speak to my father."

"Of course. What's the problem?" Marshall noticed she was a little hesitant. "Well, my dad is home and he is paralyzed by fear. All of a sudden, he cannot do his work. He's a successful businessman, but now he won't leave his house."

"Does he know Jesus?"

"No, sir, I don't believe he does."

Marshall, ever eager to share the good news of Jesus with others, said, "Of course I'll go see him."

"Pastor Brandon," Ina said, "there's something you need to know."

Marshall looked at her, wondering what could be worse than not knowing the Lord. "My dad, Dan, is a racist. He hates Black people. I'm not sure what he'll do, but he has given me his permission to ask you to come see him."

Oh boy, here we go again. Lord, I know you've sent me here for Your purposes, and this is one. Help me show nothing but love to this man.

"That's okay, Ina," Marshall said. "God can break the strongest human barriers. Let's see what He does with your dad."

A few days later, Marshall went to Dan's house.

Lord, lead me as I speak to this man. Let me get out of the way and You speak through me. That's all I ask. And please don't let him shoot me when he sees I am a Black man.

Dan invited Marshall in and was, to Marshall, surprisingly cordial. In his PJs, Dan was seated in a wheelchair. Once a day-trader, Dan had fallen into deep anxiety about the constant flux of the stock market. His doctors placed him on a defibrillator that malfunctioned; it kept shocking him. Dan told Marshall about his career success story and how he became so anxious, he took early retirement from work.

Marshall shared how Dan could gain the peace of Jesus through the power only the Holy Spirit can give. Then he asked, "Do you want that peace, Dan?"

"Yessir, I sure do."

Marshall led him in the prayer of salvation, and everything changed for Dan. He started attending church and went back to work filled with peace. Two years later, Dan became terminally ill, and Marshall was privileged to visit and pray for him. Dan knew his time was short, and he asked Marshall to officiate at his funeral, which Marshall was honored to do.

———

A few weeks in a row, Marshall saw the same man in the church atrium each Sunday. He stood out to Marshall because he appeared to be from India, and Marshall was happy to see diversity growing within the church. He didn't know him, but he caught the man staring. The man would look away and then walk in another direction as Marshall approached. On the third week, the man came into the church office during the week to see Marshall. Unfortunately, he came on Marshall's day off. Marshall's assistant called him and told him he needed to see this man as soon as possible. She related that she thought he seemed in a dark place, maybe even suicidal.

Marshall told her to call him back and tell him he would come in that same day and meet with him. As soon as Marshall came in, he recognized him as the man he had seen in the atrium. As the tall man came into Marshall's office, Marshall could tell he was broken. He wept and could barely talk. Marshall listened and encouraged him to continue.

He told Marshall his story. "Sin is overwhelming my life."

Marshall was intrigued that this young man knew the definition of sin.

"My marriage is in deep trouble, and my wife is about to leave me. I am at the end."

Marshall considered it a profound privilege to listen and talk with him. He said, "You have hope in Jesus Christ. He is a Savior who loves you and can do exceedingly abundantly above all that we ask or think."

The shattered man looked at Marshall with bloodshot eyes marked by his anguish.

Marshall felt God's peace overwhelm him and said, "This is between you and God. Do you want to pray to receive Christ as your Savior? You need to do it because you *want* to, not because I am coercing you to. Do you believe that what I've shared with you is true, that Jesus indeed is the Christ?"

"Oh, yeah! I want to be saved! What do I do?"

Marshall asked him to take a few days to think about it, but he refused. He wanted to pray immediately. Marshall got up from his seat behind his desk, walked around, and stood over him, ready to lead him in the prayer of salvation. The young man dropped to his knees, weeping, and fiercely hugged Marshall's legs.

"Lord Jesus, I believe You came and died for me. I believe You were resurrected and now sit at the right hand of God the Father. Please forgive me for my many sins. I want You to be my Lord and Savior, and I want to be cleansed from all my sins. Please save me, Lord Jesus."

Marshall saw an instant change in him. As the already tall man stood, he seemed to have gained six inches. Marshall called his assistant and said what she would understand meant a newly saved soul sat in his office, "Lisa, please bring me a Bible." When she brought it, they all whooped it up and danced for joy. Marshall signed the Bible for him and gave the new believer some Kingdom-building homework.

Marshall asks all new believers to read the book of John, so they can get to know Jesus. He only gave the man a short portion of the book to read, but when they met the following week, he had read the whole Gospel of John and was full of questions.

Soon his marriage was restored, and his daughters were enrolled in a Christian school. His mother, a former devout Hindu, has since given her heart to Jesus. The young man's heart for the Lord and His Word grew so much he changed vocations. He ministered for years with an apologetics ministry, sharing his testimony.

Marshall loves seeing the multiplication of the Gospel and what God can do through one life. As the Bible says, "There is joy in the presence of the angels of God over one sinner who repents" (Luke 15:10, NKJV).

Next, to set some records straight. . . .

———

The years 1999 and 2000 were auspicious for Marshall. As he settled into his new role as a pastor, he kept tabs on friends from prison. Through the ministry he started at HCC to visit correctional facilities, he corporately shared the Gospel. Individually, he met regularly with a few guys who did time with him at the OSR. One guy told him he had his record cleared, expunged. Marshall started thinking about having the same thing done.

The process for expungement begins with the former felon filing an application with the court where the crime took place. Once Marshall filled out his form, the investigation began. The court sent people to talk to Marshall's family in Youngstown and his immediate family in Akron. They also sent people to talk to Marshall's employers, pastoral friends, and creditors. The whole process existed to see how he lived and interacted in society since being paroled and to verify what he had written on his application.

The vetting process took about eight weeks. On a sunny, warm day in late spring of 2000, Katika and a family friend, Ed, accompanied Marshall to his hearing before the judge in Youngstown, the seat of Mahoning

County. Ed is a longtime friend as well as a businessman who conducts his affairs with godly wisdom. As Marshall entered the courtroom, he vividly remembered the last time he stood in this courthouse. He felt chilled and warm all at the same time. The judge was White, but to Marshall, she just looked stern. She looked at Marshall with eyes he swore could see right through him, and she held a large sheaf of papers.

Lord, this woman may be White, but You love her, and because of Your love, I love her too.

God turned Marshall's immediate distrust of White men into compassion. *Lord, I lay this all out before You, just as I did when I asked Jesus to be my Lord and Savior.*

"Mr. Brandon," the judge said, "we've taken the time to investigate your goings-on since you were paroled."

His military training still intact, Marshall stood straight and said, "Yes, ma'am."

"I can see as I look through the interview transcripts that you have been very busy since 1973. Is there anything you'd like to add that would clarify what I've been reading?"

Oh my, Marshall thought as he stood before the judge. He looked back at Katika and Ed and smiled.

Thank You, Lord, for giving me this opportunity to share what You have been doing in my life.

Marshall looked back at the judge. "Your Honor, ma'am," Marshall began, "when I got out of prison, I got to go to college. That's where I met my wife, Katika. I was able to complete three years of college and was married to this fine woman. But even with those positives, it didn't take long for me to fall back into addiction. Because of that, I cared little for anything else but how to get my daily drugs."

"But you didn't end up back in prison, right?" the judge asked.

"No, ma'am, I had a few days in city jail, but my new prison time came about because of the drugs. I didn't finish school, I abused my wife's trust, and she left me. *That's* the prison I found myself in. I was at an end, Your Honor, and I was lost in an abyss I couldn't dig myself out of. But Katika was so gracious, so kind; she got saved and invited me to church."

The judge didn't stop him for questions; she sat and listened.

"In 1977, after going to church with Katika for a while, I became a Christian. I prayed and confessed my many sins to God. I proclaimed Him as my Lord and Savior and thanked Him for saving my sorry hind end . . ." Marshall blanched. "Sorry, Your Honor."

The judge chuckled and said, "Please continue, Pastor Brandon."

"Thank you. After I got saved, I wanted to go straight into ministry, you know, be a pastor. But the Lord had other ideas. I worked for Ohio Edison for seventeen years as I became more involved in my church. I became a deacon and started a prison ministry."

The judge said, "Really? You chose to go back into the halls that held you captive for so long?"

"Your Honor," Marshall said, "how can I not go back in and tell the other men about how God saved me and changed me? My favorite hymn is 'Amazing Grace,' Your Honor. Those men are blind, just as I was, and I feel it's my obligation and privilege to share Jesus with them so they too can see. I am a wretch, your honor, but I am a saved wretch."

"That's a wonderful way to serve," the judge said.

"I thank God for the ability to do it. After I left Ohio Edison, I went to work for the Haven of Rest homeless mission. I loved ministering both to the men and the staff. Then I was given the chance to go to Hudson Community Chapel as a pastor. In addition to continuing my prison ministry, I get to share the Bible's vision of unity in diversity, starting in the church. My belief is that everything good should come out of the church."

The judge looked thoughtfully at Marshall. "Mr., or rather, Pastor Brandon, it is my privilege to grant you this expungement. I hope that what I see in you—the changes for the better—will come about in many others because of what you are doing. I see so many who do not change; it is a real pleasure to see a life changed and well-lived. I wish we saw more people like you come through here."

Marshall wanted to yell a sweet hallelujah, but he restrained himself.

"Your Honor, thank you both for your time and for listening to how God is working in my life. Thank you for granting me this expungement."

Lord, You expunged my record on the cross. I thank You for granting me this too. Is there anything too hard for You?

CHAPTER TWENTY

SOMEPLACE TO FINALLY BE SOMEBODY

Marshall Brandon now looks at the world and knows what to expect of it. He knows God is in the saving business. What we have in this world is temporal; what we have with Christ is eternal.

He loves to talk about giving our lives to eternal things because God is forever on His throne. Marshall often shares, "We are moving toward the culmination of the world, and God will send Jesus after His church. We get to spend eternity with Him! No more sickness, no more death. New bodies! Whoo!"

Marshall got to go to South Africa twice and to Venezuela eight times on short-term mission trips. As impactful as each trip before, his sweetest mission trip was to Vietnam in 2006. As he prepared with his team, he bore a confluence of emotions—joy at the thought of going back and reticence too. He kept his nervousness mostly to himself, sharing only with his wife.

When the day arrived to leave for Vietnam, Marshall pushed himself to take a calm walk through the airport to the team's gate. He wanted to sprint. As they boarded, he sat in the aisle seat he had requested. When Marshall flies, he usually requests a window seat to enjoy the view, so he pondered why he changed his habit on this trip. Maybe looking out at the passing ocean and landscape would prove too much for his tender emotions. Remembering the past in his mind's eye seemed the safest way for him to travel back to Vietnam after so many years. As the plane approached their destination, he prayed for a closure of past wounds. Every emotion his memories mustered—anxiety, excitement, dread, joy—all formed a confused mixture. This time he arrived in Vietnam on a blessed, different mission. When he landed in 1966, he carried rage and a gun; this time he carried forgiveness, love, and a Bible. When the plane touched down, it took all he had to stay in his seat. Yet as the leader of this group of short-term missionaries, he wanted to show proper deportment and care for the other members of the team. But this was so personal, his emotions so raw.

As a young man, he saw Vietnam through the eyes of an eighteen-year-old who harbored deep-seated anger. He sought to assuage his anger by serving his country as his heroes had done. But the abuse and hostility directed at him as a Black man only intensified his anger. Back then, he wanted to beat those who abused him, just as his mom had beaten any joy out of him.

Forty years later, he disembarked as a new creation in Christ, eager to share what the Lord did in his life. Marshall wanted to share how God could change the lives of the people He gave him to meet. As he and his team walked down the steps onto the tarmac, he nearly burst with excitement. This sojourn completed his transformation. He felt closure to his experiences as a young man intent on doing nothing for the Lord. Now, as a mature Christian—a pastor—he wanted to do *everything* for Him.

His pulse raced and his senses took in all that awaited them. God closed that early chapter of his life. He allowed Marshall to remember where he came from, but He just as graciously bid him shake off the past to complete the task at hand. Where before he had experienced only resentment and abuse, he now saw the joy of opportunity. He stood with a firm countenance on the ground where he had formerly been taken hostage by the evils of war, abuse, and addiction.

Thank You, Lord, for making me new. Thank You for making me Yours!

Marshall no longer worried about finding someplace to be somebody. That was for the old Marshall—the one that departed when he accepted Christ as his Savior. He was and is now involved in the Kingdom of the

Almighty—someplace to be somebody for God's glory—and he knows he will never retire from his calling. He chuckled to himself as he stood on the tarmac. *Lord, I know I won't retire until You take me home. Thank You, Jesus!*

As the good Lord calmed his emotions, he looked at his group and said, "Let's meet our contact. We have the Lord's work to do."

EPILOGUE

Whatever you do, work heartily, as for the Lord and not for men, knowing that from the Lord you will receive the inheritance as your reward.

You are serving the Lord Christ (Colossians 3:23-24).

On August 12, 2017, an attack on counterdemonstrators, to protests involving both the Klan and other White supremacy groups, injured more than thirty people and killed one young woman. They were struck by an automobile driven by 20-year-old James Alex Fields, a supporter of Nazi and White supremacy groups. Marshall preached Sunday, August 20, not long after that horrific racial clash in Charlottesville, Virginia.

A tense multicultural crowd filled the sanctuary. Many sat on the edges of their seats, singing with the worship team and keeping their eyes on Pastor Brandon, who stood in the front row, arms raised as he praised his Lord and Savior. The worship team concluded their last song. As Marshall mounted the steps to the platform, the congregation still stood, waiting for him to speak. They applauded for a long time on this emotional morning.

This excerpt of the message he shared is a fitting epilogue to his memoir.

———

I come with a heavy heart this morning, especially as a man of color because of all that's going on.

I prayed some years ago that God would make sure I am never insensitive to what goes on in the world—that He would break my heart with whatever breaks His. That is still my prayer. We live in a broken world, but we are not left without hope. As believers, we have hope in a God who shows up. We have more hope for the world than the world has for itself. We have to look at the living Word, Jesus Christ, because He has not left us without help or instruction. We don't have to figure it out on our own. He gives us help so that we might glean from it, follow it, and obey it.

We gather to worship the Lord through song, the written Word, and through the testimony of a God who's alive and well, enabling us to do exceedingly abundantly above all we can ask or think. We have a God who is able!

Marshall leaned in toward the congregation. Forehead veins enlarged, he continued.

"Charlottesville."

He paused, trying to keep his emotions in check.

There are photos on Facebook—photos of police brutality and Black men beat down.

I'm telling you, as a Black man, that bothers me. It has bothered me for a long time.

When I was a young, unsaved man, I wanted to do something about it. I wanted to be violent. I wanted to fight! But then I met Jesus.

His veins no longer popping, he relaxed his shoulders and looked up. Numerous amens rose from the people.

He changed my heart, and He changed my life. Where I used to have hate, I now have love in its place. Because of Jesus and who He is and what He is able to do. He changes everything!

"Preach it, brother," one person after another said.

"When Martin Luther King Sr. died in 1984, he was eulogized as the Father of the Civil Rights Movement in America. Some Black folks said, "If we started our own country, he would be our George Washington." In his eighty-four years, he endured more than his share of suffering and hatred. During his childhood in Georgia, he experienced a lot of injustice, and he even witnessed lynchings.

The first time he tried to register to vote in Atlanta, he found that the registrar's office was on the second floor of City Hall, but the elevator was marked *Whites Only*. The stairwell was closed, and the elevator for Blacks was out of order.

He is mostly remembered for the accomplishments of his son, the Rev. Martin Luther King Jr.—leader of the nonviolent civil rights movement, cut down by an assassin's bullet in 1968. One year later, Martin Luther King Sr.'s second son, Alfred Daniel (A. D.) King, drowned in a backyard swimming pool. The crowning blow came in 1974 during a church service with the loss of his wife, Alberta Williams King. As she played "The Lord's Prayer" on the church's new organ, a young man arose in the congregation, drew two pistols, and began shooting. Mrs. King collapsed and died in a hail of gunfire.

Near the end of his life, reflecting on the loss of his wife and his oldest son, he spoke of the policy of nonviolence he had come to embrace. Here's what he had to say:

There are two men I am supposed to hate. One is a White man, the other is Black, and both are serving time for having committed murder. I don't hate either one. There is no time for that and no reason either. Nothing that a man does takes him lower than when he allows himself to fall so low as to hate anyone.

It's hard enough when you see injustice done to others. But when it hits your own family, can you imagine? What are you supposed to do? It seems natural and even proper to hate killers and fight back, doesn't it? Rev. King's answer comes back: "There is no time for that." To hate is to live in the past, to dwell on deeds already done.

The truth about hatred is that it is the least satisfying emotion, for it gives the person you hate a double victory, once in the past, once in the present.

No time to hate. Not if you have learned how to forgive. Hear me now, forgiving does not mean whitewashing the past, but it does mean refusing to live there. Forgiveness breaks the awful chain of bitterness and the insidious desire for revenge. As costly as it is to forgive, there is only one consolation—unforgiveness costs far more.

Behind our anger lies a problem we rarely talk about and therefore rarely face. We have wrongly judged another person and have sinned in the process. In our rush to judgment—in our haste to make sure someone else takes the blame—in our zeal to find the guilty party, we have violated the words of Jesus in Matthew 7:1, "Judge not, that you be not judged."

We are not in the condemning business. If anyone needs to be condemned, God Himself can take care of that. We should have no part in it. Ask God to help, to empower us to do what we are to do. We can look at the fruit. We judge a tree by its fruit. We ought to have some works that identify us as believers. People ought to see that in us too!

We are so wicked by nature that we don't know why we do what we do. Some of us can remember times when we did or said something foolish, and looking back, we can honestly say, "I don't know why I did something stupid like that."

We think about things like Charlottesville. Let me tell you. God works all things together for good! He is alive and He changes things and is still transforming hearts.

As I have been thinking about this topic all week long, one thing has bothered me. I see far too much of this in my own life. If I am honest with myself, I know that I'm far too quick to pass judgment on others, and that makes me very uneasy.

The apostle Paul perfectly described this sort of attitude in words we have all heard many times: "Love is patient and kind, love does not envy or boast, it is not arrogant or rude. It does not insist on its own way, it is not irritable or resentful, it does not rejoice at wrongdoing, but rejoices with the truth. Love bears all things, believes all things, hopes all things, endures all things" (1 Corinthians 13:4-7).

Where do we go from here? "Daddy King" was right. We have no time to hate, no time to condemn, no time to live in bitterness. We need the help of God to do a supernatural work in our hearts. This isn't natural! It's SUPERnatural. We must worship Him in Spirit and in truth. Lead in loving! Lead in being kind. Be quick to forgive, restore someone, help someone struggling with sin.

It's what we are saying to Charlottesville.

We've got hope in Jesus Christ!

I'd like to suggest a simple prayer for the Holy Spirit to take over your life. Saying words alone won't change your heart, but if these words reflect your deepest desire, then today could be a new beginning for you.

"Heavenly Father, our problem is not with your Word. We know what it says. And our problem is not with other people, not even the ones who have hurt us deeply. Our problem is on the inside. For too long we have tried to solve our own problems, and it has not worked. We confess that too many times we have been critical of those around us. Forgive us our thoughtless, unkind, hurtful words. O Lord, show us a better way! Without you, we will never change. Lord Jesus, thank You for showing us how to live. Thank You for showing us how to forgive the people who have hurt us the most.

"Holy Spirit, fill us with Your power so that we might become truly different people. Set us free from bitterness, from anger, and from a judgmental spirit. Grant us power to love each other.

"Make us like Jesus, full of grace and truth. And do it now, in this moment, as we pray this prayer. Amen."

May God grant you new life through Christ in the power of the Holy Spirit. And may you experience the freedom of forgiveness and the joy that comes from letting Him take control.

Come, Lord Jesus. Even so, come!

Amen.

LOOKING BACK, LOOKING FORWARD

by Lisa Loraine Baker

It has been a prayer of ours that what we have written in *Someplace to Be Somebody* gives a true representation of Marshall's life as seen through his perspective. We have also prayed that God will get the glory through the distribution of this book.

As I carried the box with the completed manuscript to Marshall and Tik's house, I admit a feeling of trepidation. We had discussed many aspects of the book as I wrote it, and I thought I would cause Marshall to "go Youngstown" on me a few times as I peppered him with questions that dug deeper into the past that he would ofttimes rather forget. But with the grace given him by the Lord, he answered my every query with patience and detailed candor. I wanted what they read and fact-checked to be as true as the Lord would have it. And, yes, I wanted their approval—all three— the Lord, Marshall, and Tik. We want that truth of how God worked and continues to work in their lives to jump off the pages and cause people to accept Jesus as Lord and give Him all the praise.

After we went through the manuscript, which, thankfully, had few errors, Marshall and Tik and I sat together to reflect on God's story in Marshall and Tik's lives. What follows is a look back at added remembrances and a view of how the Lord is currently working in them.

LOOKING BACK AT RUTHIE

Katika: I view my mother-in-law as a strong, Black woman who came out of abject poverty and was limited by a society that didn't value her, a Black woman. I'm not going to say racist, but we weren't necessarily valued by the main White culture—the dominant culture. That trickled down into our culture, where you're not respected, and with some, it trickled down as "We're just chattel."

With my mother-in-law, I felt she had so many obstacles to have to overcome because educating her was not a priority in her family. It wasn't that she was stupid because she wasn't. She did the best she could, and she was very resourceful with what she did have with her limited education.

I felt that she chose *not* to be a victim, so she was a fighter. That fighting came out in a number of different ways, both for her dignity or whatever else it was that she held dear. Sometimes it ended up directed at her children or her husband as she fought for what she thought would give her happiness.

In the seven or so years that I got to know her, Ma Brandon had mellowed out and was always kind and gracious to me. I know what happened in Marshall's childhood, and I do not want to minimize that. But I think you need to know I viewed her as a strong, Black woman who had to fight against all the adversity she had thrown at her.

I think that's why it's important for us to realize she was strong, although far from perfect. Some of that strength manifested itself in some not so-good-ways, obviously, but she was always great with me. And although I knew that side was in her, I never saw it. I was sad to lose her when she died.

Marshall: My mom and I, we had a love. I know she loved me, and there was nothing I couldn't get from her. If I needed it and she had it, she gave it, even when I was in prison. She sent me a cake while I was in Nam! It was all busted and a mess, but what a gift. Mom was a protector, even with the dichotomy that she was hard on me.

She handled the household because Dad never did. She did day work too! She cleaned houses to help make ends meet. We didn't have much, but I had pride in how she kept our clothes cleaned and ironed.

MARSHALL'S REACTION TO THE BOOK

Reading the book has caused me to recount so many emotions and realize I have been affected by PTSD, which I denied for so many years. I had it from the abuse, Nam, prison, and addiction. Reading this changed my mood so many times because it was hard to look back at the earlier years. It's an easier read for me once we get to the Vietnam section and beyond. And I love it when we get to the good part where I got saved!

MARSHALL'S AND KATIKA'S SEPARATION

Katika: I called the police on Marshall more than a few times. One time they came and told me to leave my own apartment. *My* house! He didn't bully his way in; he was pleasant and kind. I opened the door for him not out of fear but because he presented himself as nonthreatening and said he just wanted to come by and check on me. He was a nice guy, even with the former physical abuse.

I never viewed myself as a victim and would not want to be portrayed as one. I left him two or three times, one time for three weeks, until the final time. I had no idea how strung-out Marshall was. I had no idea about his opioid addiction.

When I surrendered my life to Christ, a weight had been lifted off me. I knew I needed to share my experience with him as best I could because I knew Jesus was the answer for him as He was for me. My concern was Marshall was on the path to killing himself or at least going back to prison. At that particular point in our lives, I had a love for him, and I cared, but

I didn't like him, I didn't respect him, and I didn't trust him.

I knew he needed the Lord. I wasn't interested in reconciling with him. That wasn't my purpose. It was because I knew he needed the peace that only Jesus can give. I felt compelled to ask him to come to church with me.

LOOKING FORWARD

Marshall: This story is much bigger than we could fit in this book. We will have the Lord lead us as to what's next. It doesn't end because God has so much happening now. Because of some adversity in my life in the past few years, God has drawn Tik and me closer to each other and to Him. Katika and I are co-ministers to the people God has put into our lives. We do everything from officiating marriages to pre- and post-marital counseling. We each have mentees and we are probably as busy as a couple as we have ever been in ministry.

We love God and people. I appreciate Tik in this season of our lives—her wisdom and insight and perspective.

When I was a pastor, she supported me in that way, but this is more "us." We have a Bible study now that's so much like a house church—at least we did pre-COVID. We fill this house with twenty-plus people each week.

God has continued to show Himself faithful with ongoing opportunities for me since my "retirement'" from Hudson. For me, personally, I have been able to help minister to those affected by the opioid crisis in our area. God delivered me out of it and my heart is broken over all of this. I started a Celebrate Recovery ministry at my former church in Highland Square and also helped another organization that ministers to those affected by this crisis.

A man I know started a detox and treatment facility in February 2018. He told me I'd be great at that job. I have been given the freedom to share the Gospel in a group session each week. It's a very dark place of hurting, and I get to bring light into it. I am so thankful that more than forty men have given their hearts to Christ in my time there. God has used my past to help others going through the same things.

Marshall starts each day with this prayer:

"Lord, I thank you for a new day and new mercies.
You are so faithful.
I surrender every atom in my body to You.
Please direct my steps today so that I might tell somebody about You.
Help me to love You more today than I did yesterday."

ACKNOWLEDGEMENTS
FROM MARSHALL BRANDON

My sincere thanks are first and foremost to Jesus Christ my Lord and Savior.

To my family, for memories both good and bad that, in the end, taught me the value of home, culture, and family.

To Katika, my wife, who understood the challenges I had before me of retelling this story. With her wise counsel, she helped me tell it in the way that kept my voice both focused and true in what God would have me to share. I don't have adequate words to express the blessing she has been to me on this journey.

In the telling of this story, the one deserving my great appreciation is Lisa Baker, who framed this narrative and told it in the most reflective and simple way. She worked hard and encouraged me to make this book a reality. I could tell when she wrote it, she had good grasp of what I was trying to recall of those years.

Finally, to all of you who have loved me and encouraged me in this journey.

You know who you are. I love you.

ACKNOWLEDGEMENTS
FROM LISA BAKER

Writing for God's glory cannot be done solo. Every idea, every stroke of the keyboard is led by faith and my love of the Lord. It all begins and ends with Him—it's all for Jesus. By His grace, He brings others alongside to finish what He started. *He* gets the firstfruits!

To Stephen: I love you. God brought us to each other in His perfect timing. Thank you for loving Jesus first; that's made ALL the difference. You bring balance and completeness that has allowed me to be the person God made me to be. Life with you is a daily miracle. Happy wife!

To Marshall: In God's providence—His timing—He made this all come together. Thank you (and Tik) for loving me and for trusting me with God's story in your life. I've never done such hard, fruitful work, and, though I've read through it many times, I still laugh and cry at certain parts and love you both even more. What a testimony! What a God!

To Diane, Keli, Jenn, and Drew: You've loved me through this and learned more than you ever thought about this crazy writing business. From my heart, thank you. I love you.

To T (Tampa): The friend I called to help me with the huge, coach decision. Your immediate "Do this!" gave me the confidence I needed to press on. You are loved!

To Tonya: Your prayers have helped carry me through. You rock and you know how much I love you!

To Ginger: From coach to friend. No way would this have come together as it has without your inspired leadership. Thank you!

To Jim Rubart: Yeah, it's not so much a Writing Academy as it is a Life Academy! Your mentorship and friendship face me toward the Lord and His plans for me. From my heart, thank you!

To Victoria Duerstock, Bethany Jett, Cyle Young, Del Duduit, Michelle Medlock Adams: What an amazing, godly group of creatives. Vicki, you took a chance because you know the story, and you know it needs to be out there so God can use it to change lives. Bethany and Michelle, your inspired teaching and encouragement make me not only a better writer, but a better person who strives to proclaim the Lord in all I do. Cyle, you oversee all your agents and clients with diligence and prayer. It means more than I could ever express through mere words.

To my incredible Monketeers (Jeannie Waters, Jean Wilund, Julie Lavender, and Lori Hatcher). Oh, how we love, push, pray, humble, laugh, and encourage each other. I am a better person because of "all y'all!"

Janis Whipple: You helped me tighten and clarify this story so it shines even brighter. My heartfelt thanks!

To Eva Marie Everson (Word Weavers, Int'l.): The breadth of your leadership is deep and wide, and you've helped direct this writer's life toward excellence and authenticity. Thank you.

To the unnamed but deeply loved, thank you.

Soli Deo gloria!